MAXIMUM
Entertainment

Director's Notes
for
Magicians and Mentalists

Ken Weber

Maximum Entertainment
Director's Notes for Magicians and Mentalists
by Ken Weber

ISBN 0-9746380-0-5
Printed and bound in the United States of America

First Edition, 2003

Published by:

Ken Weber Productions
1983 Marcus Ave. #221
Lake Success, NY 11042
www.ken-weber.com
maxent@ken-weber.com

Layout by Mark Garetz www.creationary.com

Acknowledgments

As with any good piece of magic, there is more to getting a book published than meets the eye. The process requires a team, and I was fortunate to have an "A" team on board.

Bob Baker, Doug Dyment, Mark Sherman, and John Sherwood offered continuous encouragement and then polished, corrected and kneaded this book into the product you now hold. Each, to varying degrees, is a wordsmith, each has extensive performing experience, and they provided invaluable assistance.

I also want to acknowledge Kathy Daly for the time she stole from her professional and home life to help with the proofreading.

Mark Garetz assumed the arduous task of morphing my electronic bits and bytes into a physical, well-designed book.

My sincere thanks to them all.

And special hugs and kisses to Neela, Melanie and Daryl, who care not one bit about anything in this book; they are the perfect balance in my life.

Dedicated to Gil Eagles,
who taught me the magic of sharing.

Foreword

By Bob Baker

When Ken Weber talks, the top mystery entertainers in the world listen. When Ken Weber advises, professional mentalists who earn hundreds of thousands of dollars a year take his advice. Why? Because Ken Weber knows how to make a performance entertaining, and to the most successful magicians and mentalists in the world, maximizing entertainment is what matters the most.

It's also what matters the most to our audiences. Frankly, it's the only thing that matters to them. But how do we learn to truly entertain an audience? We do hundreds or thousands of shows, learn from our mistakes, and, over time, we get better. However, wouldn't it be wonderful if a great coach could help us accelerate this process? An expert entertainer to watch us perform, point out our errors, and show us what to do to perfect our acts. A director. A mentor. A friend. In this book, Ken Weber can fill these roles for you.

Ken, of course, didn't start his performing career at the top of his profession. Like many of us New York performers, he began in the humble bungalow colonies of New York's Catskill Mountains—the Borscht Belt. I first became aware of Ken's existence when he and I were paying our performing dues there in the 1970s. (Performing dues: a 1:00 A.M. show in a non-air conditioned "rec" hall for a hostile crowd just back from a losing night at Monticello Racetrack.) In those days Ken and I trod the same boards, but for me to say we were competitors would be blatant self-aggrandizement.

As Ken perfected his show, his career leapt forward, and, until he made a major career change (more on that later), Ken was one of the top mentalists/hypnotists in North America. I've had the pleasure of seeing Ken perform many times. I've seen him turn a restless crowd of a thousand cynical college kids into a stomping, cheering audience convulsed with laughter; I've also marveled as he performed under the toughest of conditions and turned what would have been disaster for most performers into another successful show.

That's why, when the Psychic Entertainers Association wanted a performer's performer to conduct an open critique of the professional mentalists who had entertained at the PEA's annual convention, they turned to Ken.

What? Critique your peers? Publicly? Was the guy nuts? Well, that's what we all thought, but Ken pulled it off magnificently. So much so that he has been invited to repeat his seminar many times since. But while Ken was teaching others, he was also learning. He studied other performers. He saw a myriad of ways to help even the best entertainers improve. And then he decided to write it down. You hold the result in your hands.

In this book, Ken gives you tools and techniques that will enable you to advance from being a good performer to a great one. You will benefit from his twenty-five years of performing experience before every conceivable type of audience. You will discover in a single reading what most magicians and mentalists never learn in a lifetime.

Now, you may be wondering, "If this guy is so great, how come I've never heard of him?" Maybe it's because you've never seen any of his thousands of college or corporate shows. It might also be because Ken does not work magic conventions, lecture to magic clubs, or pontificate in magic magazines. (Frankly, he's too busy managing several hundred million dollars of other people's money—his profession since retiring from full-time performing.) But the fact that you don't know Ken Weber doesn't mean you can't learn something from him. And this is whether you're an amateur performer or a working pro.

Who knows? If I'd known way back when what I've learned from Ken since, I might not have ended up as a physician.

So get ready to discover the real secrets of magic. You are about to hear from a master performer, expert analyst, and all-around nice guy. Read, study, and learn. Apply what Ken teaches, and watch the change in the way your spectators respond to your magic.

You have nothing to lose but your audience.

Contents

Section I

◄ PREAMBLE ►

*"The introduction to a document
that serves to explain its purpose."*

Honesty…
hardly ever heard,
but mostly what I need.

Billy Joel

Introduction

One of the most successful mentalists in the world begins his show with a warm-up exercise to "get his mind in gear." He calls it "Mental Calisthenics." Except that, for a time, he pronounced it "cal-is-*thet*-ics."

The tradition in most performing arts says that we always stroke a performer after a show, and save our true feelings for ourselves—or we share them with others and leave the performer no wiser.

I've grown weary of that mindset. I love my craft too much.

We sink or swim together. Bad magic and weak mentalism smear all magicians and mentalists. And surely the opposite is true; successful performers increase demand for the genre.

The mentalist in this story is a dear friend. With some trepidation I told him about his mispronunciation. At first he was sure I was mistaken. After all, he holds advanced university degrees and had been saying that line for years.

"Are you sure?" he asked again with a combination of skepticism and worry.

"Yes, I'm certain," I replied, not knowing whether I was stepping over some ego-proscribed line.

"Calisthenics. Calisthetics." He said them both several times. Then he looked directly at me, put his hand on my shoulder, and said, "Thanks, Ken." He knew that wasn't easy for me and he wanted to make it clear he was grateful.

That one word was an infinitesimally small moment within a masterful one-hour presentation, but as working pros know, every moment counts, and we can always raise the level of our show.

The friendship endured, and I woke up to the need for sharing—rather than hiding—our honest opinions. My purpose within these pages is to look at the small moments (and some larger issues as well) that raise or lower the level of your performance.

Traditional magic books, videos, and catalogues give you the mechanics of the tricks. This book examines the other elements that comprise a successful entertainment experience: the cement between the bricks.

Teen Magazine Advice

When I was sixteen years old, I wrote up a card trick that appeared in a magazine for teenage magicians. I urged the readers of my simple little trick to "make it entertaining." It's not that I knew what that meant, but I had seen the phrase written by so many others that I assumed it was mandatory.

From the day you began reading your first magic book, you have been repeatedly reminded that your job is to *entertain* your audience.

"Your tricks must be entertaining."

"Don't forget, you are an entertainer."

Entertain... entertainment... entertaining... entertainer.

Blah, blah, blah. Easily written, rarely defined, those admonitions appear in our literature so often they have evolved into vapid clichés.

But what exactly *is* entertainment? Specifically, what makes one trick entertaining and another merely a boring puzzle? What actions, gestures, or words levitate a conjuring trick into something recognized as entertainment? And equally important, what specifically *detracts* from the entertainment experience?

In other words, *how* do you achieve entertainment? Those are the questions we tackle in this book. And we'll do it, at some points, in great detail.

Ken Who?

You probably don't know me. You've never seen my name in a major magic publication, and I am not clever enough to have invented any commercial tricks. I'm including a brief autobiography here for two reasons. Primarily, since I'm offering advice—sometimes delivered bluntly—this book may have more credence for you if you understand my background: my qualifications as an "expert." Knowing that I've managed to achieve a significant level of success as an entertainer may allow the medicine to go down more easily. Secondly, I enjoy reading other stories about "a life in magic," and would like to think that you feel the same. So please allow me to introduce myself.

I'm a native New Yorker, but from ages ten through twelve I lived in a home for asthmatic children in Denver, Colorado. Back then, the mid-1950s, asthma was a fairly rare and highly misunderstood disease, and one theory held that it has a strong psychosomatic component. That approach, since discredited, posited that parents might inadvertently be a trigger for the attacks, so after years of unsuccessfully trying other treatments, my parents, heartbroken, shipped me off to the foothills of the Rockies. They were allowed only two one-week visits during twenty-five months.

Sad to think back on it now, but the experience held the key, for better or worse, to my entry into show business. During the middle of that two-year stretch, while walking by myself in downtown Denver (life was different for an 11-year-old then!) I stopped at the window of a store unlike anything I had seen before. At first I thought it was a toy store but there were masks and "gags" and tricks. A young man emerged from the store and said to me, "Do you like magic?"

"Umm, I guess so."

"Well, come here next Saturday for a free magic show."

It turned out the free magic show was actually a meeting of a teenage magic club, and that afternoon changed my life. I began reading everything on magic in the local libraries (I find it curious that most magicians don't know the significance of 793.8. Hint: Ask your librarian), and by the time I moved back to New York I thought of myself as a twelve-year-old magician.

At age fifteen I first saw my name in print; *TV Guide* listed me as the *Teen-Talent* guest on the popular *Wonderama* children's show (with Sonny Fox, the host prior to magician Bob McAllister). For a few weeks during the 1964 World's Fair, I held the title of "Official Magician" at the RCA Pavilion (among others, Peter Pit and The Amazing Randi also filled that role for short periods). The RCA folks exploited my talents to help introduce color TV to the passing public. "Ladies and gentlemen," the young female tour guides intoned, "if you look through the windows down into the television studio, you'll see our magician. Now look at the TV monitors above you; notice the red of the handkerchief he's waving around? See how the red appears the same as what you see in the studio."

"Ahhh!"

Saturday afternoons during my late-teen and early-twenties years followed a pattern: First stop, Lou Tannen's store, where I'd hang out watching demonstrations of tricks that I couldn't afford, then at 3:00 P.M., when the shop closed, move with the gang to "the cafeteria" to schmooze with guys like Richard Himber, Harry Lorayne, and many others whose names I no longer recall.

My best friend in magic back then was Jeff Sheridan, the person who single-handedly brought the art of street magic back to America. Sometimes Jeff and I would leave Tannen's and just "bop" around Manhattan, practicing our latest tricks on comely females. Other times we took the subway downtown to Al Flosso's dingy shop (more about this great man in my Personal Entertainment Highlights).

One day, Jeff introduced me to a young lad who was standing at Tannen's counter, accompanied by one of his parents. The demonstrator was spending a good deal of time with the kid, a sure sign he smelled money. I could never fathom scenes like that. My parents barely tolerated my addictive hobby, and here was a kid whose parents encouraged—*encouraged*—his interest in magic! Jeff told me that not only did the folks buy tricks for that spoiled brat (that's how I viewed him and all others who came to the shop with a parent, usually just once or twice, never to been seen again), they were even paying Jeff to give him card manipulation lessons. Hah! What a waste of money.

Everyone knows—certainly I knew—that you must suffer for your art. No pain, no gain. Handing him magic on a silver platter would only soften him and make him cower once he experiences failure in front of strangers. Nonetheless, the parents kept paying and the kid diligently continued his lessons, surprising me, and as I recall, to a lesser extent, Jeff as well. Whatever became of that kid, David Kotkin?

Higher learning for me took place at Long Island's Hofstra University, where I majored in Speech and Drama. That combined major was chosen because it *a)* seemed useful to my magic career, and *b)* was easier than a real major.

It was there that I began my formal study of acting and directing. Thanks to the first-rate reputation of Hofstra's drama department, the faculty included talented people from nearby New York City. Writers, directors, and actors with Broadway experience were more than happy to sign on for steady paychecks. Those teachers showed me the collaborative nature of entertainment. And it was at Hofstra that I first experienced the technique of the director, sitting alone in the theater watching the rehearsals, taking notes.

Director's notes. One person, sitting where the audience sits, objectively observing and writing notes. One person coaching another. *It's the backbone of theater.*

After earning my Bachelor of Arts degree, I went on to Brooklyn College of the City University of New York. There, I picked up a Master's Degree in Broadcasting, and all my elective courses were again, as at Hofstra, related to either acting or directing.

During my two years time at Brooklyn College I produced and hosted what we were told was the first student-run TV program in the United States to have a regular run on a broadcast station. It was, in fact, a forerunner of MTV, with music and news strictly for young adults. Yet, despite what I considered an impressive resume, no company in TV land shared my enthusiastic opinion of me, and so I took a temp office job.

Three months later, I received the call that morphed my avocation into my profession: an agent said he could book me for two weeks performing on cruise ships. That meant quitting my steady job for the vagaries of show biz, and fostered an inner conversation regarding the pros and cons of the two choices: work in an office for people I don't like and who don't like me, or get paid twice as much to sail around the Caribbean and do magic and mentalism, but with no secure prospects afterwards.

I packed my bags.

For several years I worked with some regularity on the ships of the Royal Caribbean cruise line. Later on, I discovered that other cruise lines didn't treat their entertainers nearly as well. I was paid two to three times as much as similar acts on other lines, plus we cabaret entertainers were also treated with more respect. Not that we didn't work hard: I did two 45-minute afternoon shows, then transferred to another ship. Sometimes the transfer involved walking across a pier; other times the entertainers were put on a small private plane and whisked off to meet a ship on a different island. Regardless of the work schedule, when not performing we were no different from any paying guest on those floating luxury resorts. Not bad for a kid just out of school.

I then migrated to doing an ever-increasing number of what agents call "club dates." Despite the name, those were any type of paid one-night show for any audience. That's when I began traveling across America. It was during those years, the late 1970s, that I began developing my hypnosis show. (These days, one can supposedly learn stage hypnosis from any of several weekend courses. That's a regrettable development. My hypnosis training included courses at two local universities plus an intensive correspondence course from which I earned a Certificate in Clinical Hypnosis from the UCLA School of Medicine.)

Among the club dates was a steady diet of gigs in New York's infamous Catskill Mountains. The circuit there was comprised of hotels and bungalow colonies, which housed the most jaded audiences in the world. Most of the habitués had been going to "the mountains" forever, which in some cases meant before man learned to bake bread, and all the resorts provided a non-stop stream of entertainment. Impressing those folks required more than a smile and a clean suit. But it was also the best training ground for a young performer: you learned how to overcome apathy, extremes of temperature, outright antagonism ("You're *not* the stripper?"), and distractions of every variety. And, if you proved yourself worthy to the agents, you had the dubious honor of doing two or three shows on a Saturday night, each at a different resort.

Next followed the college circuit, where, needless to say, the audiences looked, sounded, and smelled different. Those kids had a natural affinity for my memory, mentalism, and hypnosis demonstrations, and at one point *Newsweek* magazine named me "one of the most requested" performers on the college circuit.

Now there's a funny thing about becoming a professional: when your hobby is your vocation, your perspective changes. For me, that change, over the course of a few years, was a major one. As I became more successful, I stopped going to magic conventions. I let my subscriptions to the magazines lapse. I rarely bought new books and tricks. Magic was no longer my hobby.

My focus became the business side of show business, and as a result, I felt reluctant to introduce new material into my act. That is not an incorrect strategy; every show is important for the professional, so why tinker with a winning formula? And if I was not going to bring new material into the act, why tease myself by seeing what others were offering in the shops and magazines? Why take money from my family's budget if I could not justify new magic as a business expense?

Right or wrong, that's how life went for more than a decade.

By the early 1980s, my show-biz career was on cruise control. I reached the happy point where I did virtually no advertising or soliciting for gigs; all shows were either repeat dates or from agents who knew and trusted my work.

Around 1982 I began a slow evolution to the world of investments. I used the time spent while flying from gig to gig researching what to do with my show-biz earnings, and after a few years I realized I knew quite a bit about one particular area: mutual funds. In the early 1980s I also became convinced that they were going to be the preferred investment vehicle of the future, and one day I told my wife that I was going to start writing a newsletter to help the average person invest intelligently in funds. I told her it would entail perhaps four or five days each month, and that while I didn't expect to make any money, it would help my subscribers avoid major investing mistakes, and let me feel that I've contributed something important to society. (Later on, and especially after 9/11, I came to appreciate more fully the important contributions artists and entertainers provide within a free society.)

The newsletter grew rapidly and, at its peak, had 5000 subscribers. In 1992 I established Weber Asset Management, a company dedicated to helping people invest intelligently through no-load mutual funds. I never planned to "retire" from show biz, but the success of my venture into the world of investments (within six years we zoomed into the top 10% of America's 37,000 Registered Investment Advisor firms, based on assets under management) snuck up on me and began to consume my time. Then came the day when I realized I had to begin declining offers for out-of-town shows. After spending years building up my reputation as an entertainer, it was truly painful to say "No thanks" when a distant college or agent requested my services, but I had no choice.

The one constant during those years was my affiliation with the Psychic Entertainers Association (PEA), an international organization of those with a serious and vested interest in mentalism, hypnosis, and related fields of entertainment (despite the name, most members eschew strong claims of psychic ability). For quite a while it was my only formalized connection, other than regular meetings with a few close friends, to the world of mystery entertainment.

In 1993, the PEA bestowed upon me their most prestigious honor, the Dunninger Memorial Award, "Awarded for Distinguished Professionalism in the Performance of Mentalism."

Three years after receiving that plaque, I volunteered—in a fit of altruism mixed with foolhardiness—to do a lecture at an annual PEA convention. It was to be a critique of the performers who appeared on the shows there. Most of my PEA friends thought I was a mentalist who had gone mental. To put it mildly, they tried to dissuade me. Nonetheless, I persisted, believing it could be pulled off without anyone committing an atrocity upon any of my vital organs.

During the Thursday and Friday night shows, I sat in the darkness with a pad and a pen, jotting down my thoughts about what I saw on the stage. Understand that all the performers at the PEA shows are members of a fairly restrictive organization, one which requires a demonstrated seriousness about the art of entertaining using mysteries of the mind; some members rarely appear in front of audiences, while many others are full-time entertainers.

And on a particular Saturday afternoon, I stood before this group of fellow performers and began, with trepidation, my point-by-point critique of the eight entertainers we had seen during the previous two evening shows.

The response exceeded anything I expected. Much of the membership at large offered me enthusiastic congratulations (one member wrote in to the organization's newsletter that it was "the best lecture I've ever seen, and I've been going to magic conventions for nearly fifty years!"). More importantly, the subjects of my critiques were the first to pull me aside to say, in various ways, "Thanks, I needed that."

I never volunteered to do the "workshop" again. Instead, for six out of the past seven years (as of 2003) the convention chairmen asked me to repeat it, and I did, and I take that as a verification that I provided a useful service to my fellow performers.

From the moment I accepted the responsibility of annually offering my "Performance Workshop" to the Psychic Entertainers Association, I began the process of systematically noting and analyzing the big and little things that helped or hindered performers in all branches of the magical arts. I believe that the workshops were well received, in part, because I dissected, with great specificity, what I saw on stage, seeking to eliminate the rough edges in otherwise smooth performances.

Over the past few years a number of people suggested I write a book based on my lectures. At first, the idea seemed preposterous. After all, my comments targeted specific moments in shows I had seen, and which had been seen by the attendees at my lectures. After a while, however, it became abundantly clear that certain themes of advice repeated themselves; those concepts coalesced into the framework for this volume.

But I recognize that the individuality of performers makes comprehensiveness impossible. I could pen a thousand pages and it still could not substitute for a live, knowledgeable mentor scrutinizing your particular act. Nonetheless, by reading this book, you will increase your ability to—in effect—mentor yourself. And if you should be fortunate enough to have a trusted friend or true director evaluate you, after digesting my advice you will be better equipped to accept or argue against any particular piece of advice with greater clarity and intellectual strength.

Pardon Me, Your Slip Is Showing

The subtitle for this book is, "Director's Notes for Magicians and Mentalists," for that was the genesis of this project—my "director's notes." A true stage director must report his views honestly and directly, and likewise in these pages you will encounter a bluntness rarely seen in typical magic prose. In any educational modality, specific examples always provide greater usefulness than generalities. That's why this book names names. Some will be offended. Sorry. At this stage of my life, I see no need to hide behind sweeping statements, so when I can point to a particular performer or a specific moment within an act to illustrate a line of reasoning, I do.

However, be assured that I do it always *with deep respect for my fellow entertainers.* From my earliest days of reading our literature, I realized that this is a unique and special brotherhood, spanning age, religion, race, and geography. Despite what you may infer from some of my criticisms, I love magic and mentalism and *all* those who share my enthusiasm for this art form. (Is magic an art? Of course it is; it's a subset of the performing arts.) My lectures were well received, in part, because I developed a reputation for fairness, and I know there is no performer who cannot teach *me* something.

And I need to let you in on a little secret: I will be commenting on, and offering suggestions about the performances of, a number of contemporary magicians and mentalists, including some of the most respected, and *I am intensely jealous* of each of them! I wish, deeply, that I possessed their skills. I don't, but that of course does not invalidate my observations. Each comment needs to stand on its own, apart from me, and it's up to you to decide whether I am on or off target.

Occasionally, after one of my lectures, a performer whom I reviewed would come up to me and explain in one fashion or another that "that's not what I usually do." I understand that they wanted to be seen in the best light. Who doesn't? However, for the purposes of the reviews, I could go only with what I saw. It's the same for the comments you'll read in this book. I fully recognize that I am commenting on routines that in some cases are not fully formed, routines these performers may never perform for a paying audience.

Is that fair? Yes, for several reasons. First, in general, my comments are about performances that are for sale to the magic world on DVD or videotape. As such, they are fair targets for honest commentary. Second, the performers chose to put those moments out before us; I didn't sneak into a rehearsal or a back-room session. But mostly, I made the decision to choose performances that you, the reader, can access.

Also, I use specific moments to make a general point. So, while the performance being discussed may not be an accurate representation of that particular artist's repertoire, my suggestions are aimed at magical performers generically.

Please Take Note

You should make notes about my notes. This hardcover book is not sacrosanct. It's an opinionated and sometimes borderline-rude "how to" manual. Mess it up! Talk back to me. Never pick up this volume without a pen, pencil, or highlighter in your hand. When you agree with a point, reinforce it with an underline. When you see something that resonates with your performance style or situation, dog-ear the corner. When you read a section and think, "This guy is nuts!" you'll gain further insight by committing your thoughts to the margins (which have been formatted extra wide specifically for this purpose). Writing it out helps ensure that you agree or disagree with me in a cogent, non-emotional manner.

As an admirer of the person who machetes his own path through life, I want you to rebel against any of the suggestions offered herein, but only if you can justify to yourself *why* you are breaking a rule. In other words, if I meet you in the hallway after your show and ask you why you ignored one of my edicts (don't worry, I won't), you should be able to articulate your reason for veering from my roadmap. Not for me... for you.

Do not trod your own way merely out of laziness or obstinacy; for maximum success attack the goal of entertainment in a thoughtful and methodical manner.

In advertising, they say fifty percent of every ad budget is wasted. The problem is, you never know in advance which fifty percent. Similarly, for you, much of this book will tell you things you find painfully obvious or that you have already garnered from your own experience. But again, until you read the book through, you won't unearth the golden nuggets that apply to *you*.

The "Science" of Entertainment? Never!

The art of entertainment does not lend itself to scholarly studies of empirical data. And that's as it should be; if entertainment could be quantified, the mystery would evaporate.

Entertainment is a personal experience. The delight of the moment takes place exclusively between the ears of each participant. Not on the stage, but in the brain. No two individuals experience the same concert, the same comedy act, the same movie, the same magic act. Where you sit, your preconceptions about the show, your relationships with your companions, your hearing and visual acuity, what you ate or did not eat, your general state of health and mind—all factor into the entertainment experience. And so it follows that achieving entertainment is shooting at a moving target. One size will never fit all; every audience presents new opportunities and challenges.

I try to steer clear of idealistic theorizing; I want my advice grounded in practicality. Theory has its place, but from the start I wanted this book to be well-larded with real-world advice for real-world performers at every level, from the hobbyist to the successful professional.

You will encounter many "do's" and a generous helping of "don'ts". All the "don'ts" result directly from watching the performances of professionals, or highly advanced amateurs, making the tips herein truly a set of director's notes: observations made while seeing performers do something that, if done differently, would be more effective. This is not a "here's what I saw at a magic club" checklist of errors made by neophytes, so please don't dismiss any tidbit of advice; it's here because someone who should have known better, didn't.

When I urge that you not do something, I rarely provide an alternative action or line of patter; I cannot be creative for you. Directors shape, push, and polish performances; it's usually up to others—the author, the playwright, the composer, or in this case *you*—to create.

Nothing you're about to read is pie-in-the-sky stuff written in an ivory tower; *it's all real-world*. My world and your world.

Chapter 1

The Search for Entertainment

Defining Entertainment

Baseball entertains. As do novels, cinema, concerts, and cricket matches (OK, that last one applies only to those fascinated by white-sweatered men who break for tea). And magic, done properly, entertains. These activities appear to have little in common. What, then, makes each a part of the world of entertainment?

My definition of entertainment is: *anything that purposefully transports your mind into another world.*

When you are being entertained, your mind focuses on the entertainment, and everything else recedes from your consciousness. The stronger the entertainment, the less likely it becomes that you will lose that focus. If your mind drifts back to your everyday world, the entertainment, for that moment, has failed.

Boredom, the opposite of entertainment, is a consequence of being forced into a situation beyond your control. For example, you cannot leave the classroom despite the droning professor, and it's impolite to walk out on an inept performer. So you stay. In those situations you're bored, and your mind moves on to other things.

"Being entertained," at its crux, can be defined as *paying attention.*

When you give your full attention to an engaging professor, singer, football game, movie, dancer, or magician—you are being entertained. Your overdue tax bill, your problems at work, your personal relationships, where you are going to eat after the show—none of it matters. The entertainment removes you from all that. Magical, musical, comedic, or theatrical entertainers take you out of your world and bring you, willingly, into theirs.

You have temporarily and willingly removed your consciousness from the world you inhabit daily, and placed it into this new realm, a different reality. You may cry, laugh, cringe, or gasp, but you are not thinking about anything related to your everyday existence.

At its best, entertainment enlightens, inspires, and communicates new insights about life

That's entertainment!

Looking For Entertainment in All the Wrong Places

Here's an anecdote that illustrates the elusiveness of the entertainment experience.

It happened in April 2002, while I attended a conference for investment professionals at a luxury resort in Dallas. Within a 12-hour span, I saw a young professional close-up magician and a 60-year-old grandmother whose topic was "Regulatory Issues and the Securities and Exchange Commission."

The Professional Magician vs. the Regulator. Which of those two was more entertaining? Common sense says there should be no contest. Investment advisors attend SEC "Update" sessions because we must; running afoul of their constantly shifting rules could put us out of business.

The magician appeared at the evening cocktail reception. Wearing an outfit signifying Texas saloonkeeper circa 1890—old-style white shirt, string tie, fringed black vest, Western boots—he approached five of us who were standing together and asked if anyone had a class ring. None of us did, and it stopped his presentation cold. He quipped, "Oh, so this is a group with no class."

A couple of people exchanged glances.

Then he rummaged around inside his shoulder bag and finally pulled out three scrawny and frayed pieces of rope. He performed a weak Professor's Nightmare routine, received polite applause (which I started for my fellow performer), and then moved on.

No one commented, either positively nor negatively; they just resumed their conversation as if he had never been there.

The following morning, Marianne Smyth spoke to us. Her physical appearance can charitably be described as frumpy, and her subject matter normally sends an audience into spasms of apathy.

There she stood, pacing in front of a group of several hundred high-powered business people. (How high-powered? The speaker immediately following her at this invitation-only event was the first President George Bush.)

At one particularly complex section of her talk, she slowly drawled out, "I think I'm losing some of you, but I'm *not* going to let that happen!" So, wrenching the wireless microphone from the lectern, she left the stage and walked down into the audience. She roamed up and down the aisles, looking directly into the faces of the many individuals she passed. She waved her hands; she banged on the tables where we sat taking notes.

No one could *not* pay full attention. The sheer force of her personality, fueled by her sincere certainty that "*This* is important to you!" made her a compelling speaker. She was a dynamo!

At one point, her fast-paced rhythm suddenly slowed, her voice softened to almost a whisper and she told us, "I—just—lowered—my—voice—and—I'm—talking—s-l-o-w-l-y—because—this—is—soooo—*important*."

The audience laughed at her audacity, and despite the laughter, everyone got the message. This woman knew how to control her audience with nothing more than her voice, her sincerity, and her fervent desire to communicate with us.

President Bush ("41," as he called himself, to differentiate him from his son, whom he referred to as "43") began his presentation by saying, "Wow, that's a tough act to follow!"

Why was Marianne Smyth so effective? What made her presentation so powerful that a former leader of the Free World felt compelled to provide a transition to his own talk?

First, she knew her stuff cold. Facts flowed seamlessly without notes. More important, her commitment to communicating, to teaching her audience in a meaningful way, overflowed from the stage and washed over all of us listening to her. She had all the entertainment cylinders firing: timing, enthusiasm, humor, emotion, surprise, and enlightenment.

Marianne Smyth, elderly-looking, rotund, disheveled, and a government policy wonk, entertained her audience far more effectively than the young professional magician.

That young magician had the basic tools. But he, as with so many others in our craft, focused on achieving mystery rather than entertainment. And he never had a chance to read the book you're holding. It's for him—a younger version of me—that I advance the theories and advice to follow.

Why a Director?

The off-Broadway show, *Ricky Jay: On the Stem*, showcased (to dazzling reviews from the New York press) one of the most accomplished performers on the American magical scene. Our profession recognizes Ricky Jay as a master of sleight of hand and all other things magical. And he is a storyteller extraordinaire.

Yet prominently displayed on the billboard outside the theater, and in all the ads, were the words, "Directed by David Mamet." That tells me two things. First, since David Mamet is a well-known playwright and film director, the producers know his name draws in an extra allotment of hoity-toity theatergoers and financial backing. Second, and more germane to this discourse, even as masterful a performer as Ricky Jay, with his vast storehouse of experience in all venues, feels that he benefits from the guidance of a trusted director.

Every performer needs a director. Writing in the May, 2002, issue of *The Linking Ring*, Bill Fienning built a strong case for magicians hiring a theatrical director, and I agree completely with his premise. Unfortunately, not everyone can find or afford a director. I want this book to be the next best thing: to help you become your *own* director.

No matter how clever and experienced you are, your magically jaded eyes do not see what the layperson sees. But you must assess your act from the layman's perspective. A good director takes on the role of the non-performer, views your show without preconceptions, then overlays his experience and judgment to refine and polish it.

With few exceptions, magicians and mentalists craft their acts unaided. Other performers have directors, choreographers, voice coaches, film editors, and scriptwriters to develop and refine their efforts. Plus, they have critics—serious critics, who analyze and nitpick. We don't. We have magazines that gloss over flaws and lead the cheering section, and this, over the generations, has not served us well.

The Importance of Being Videotaped

From the days when going to the theater meant sitting on benches hewn from the side of a mountain, certain performers garnered more fame than their peers. Yet prior to the invention of the motion picture, not a single performer, no matter how illustrious, ever saw himself from the audience's perspective. (Looking in a mirror doesn't count, because the moment you glance away, you can't see yourself.) Sound added another dimension, but filming was, and is still, an expensive and overly complex procedure, suitable mostly for the already established performer.

With the advent of the videocassette recorder, the ability to see what the audience sees became available to all performers. This invention, not the latest thread reel or gaffed card, is the most important breakthrough *ever* for the success of the mystery performer, and should be recognized as such.

You cannot reach your fullest potential until you critically analyze yourself on video.

Have a professional tape your show. Or have a friend do it. The specific route you take is far less important than just getting it done. Either way, it must be done unobtrusively so that the act of taping has no impact on the audience or on you.

Tape your show whenever you have a chance, and then sit down and analyze what you see, always with a pen and paper in your hands. Use this book as your manual for becoming your own director, intelligently critiquing your performance.

Among other things (which will be detailed as you progress through these pages), you want to look for a natural flow:

- of your hand movements
- of your body movements
- of your speech patterns
- of your gaze

Is there *anything* that looks awkward, out of place in any way? Any "tells"?

The best sleight of hand occurs during the off-moments. Does yours? Can it be reworked so that it does?

Watch yourself from a layman's perspective, and then watch yourself from a magician's perspective. Could you fool fellow conjurors? Does that very question strike you as silly? Your goal, I well realize, is not to fool others in our field (unless you're in a competition), but the meticulous attention to detail needed to accomplish that task will force you to confront flaws that you might otherwise too willingly overlook. So if you don't think a routine of yours could fool magicians, consider whether refining or eliminating a move, or a weak moment, would take it one step higher on the "mystifying" scale.

Typically, performers who have achieved some degree of success fight the idea of critically viewing a tape of their performance. "I hate watching myself," several have said to me. I know. I do, too. But you will have to break through that psychological barrier.

Finally, the most important aspect of videotaping yourself is the repeated viewing of the tape. The first one or two or five times you watch it, you will be watching yourself. (*My, how clever am I! And witty, too!*) Only after you pass that stage will you be able to see—dispassionately—what really happened.

Find a Mentor or a Trusted Friend

As thorough as I've tried to make this book, it can never fully replace a live human who observes and evaluates your specific performance. Each of us makes his or her own unique missteps, miscues, and mistakes. We each have blind spots for the soft spots in our acts. My goal, and yours, is to keep those weaknesses down to the barest minimum.

As magicians, we have unique needs. A theatrical director can block the action on stage for maximum effect, but in magic there is always a flaw in the action—the trick itself—the workings of which must remain undetected. So, while a theatrical director might say to an actor, "Turn to your left at that moment," if your hand is stealing a load just then, that turn to the left might be less than wise.

That's where a friend in the know helps. He's the one, and with luck the only one, who will tell you when you've flashed the coin or awkwardly palmed the card—flaws that may not be apparent even on a videotape.

This friend can serve you in one other subtle but powerful way: he can sit in your audience and overhear what people say. He can mingle unobtrusively afterward as well. The snippets he picks up, or subtly solicits, are the most real and most honest reviews possible. (Are you ready to hear what people *really* say about you? Gulp.)

Raise Your Level

From age eight to eighteen, my son Daryl actively participated in the highly competitive world of "Juniors" tennis. By age twelve he had developed all the basic strokes, and by the time he was in his late teens, and over six feet tall, he—and any of his peers—could have taken the court with any of the world-class touring pros. Daryl would not have won any games against the professional, but he could have won points, and if you had sat in the stands and watched them play just a few points, you could not have easily discerned that the pro was levels above the teenagers.

Tennis, along with many other sports, ranks players. Daryl, for example, achieved a ranking in the top 20 in the Eastern states division: a clear, specific, numerical rank. But as good as that may seem, he was ranked only around 200th nationally.

Consider, for a moment, the idea of ranking magicians with that type of specificity. Absurd? Not at all. Figure skating combines athletics and entertainment, and the judges must subjectively assign a numerical value to each performance. In theory, a panel of magic experts could do the same for our shows. As you may know, the judges at FISM and other magic competitions do in fact apply an objective set of criteria to rate the performers.

If magicians or mentalists were all given a regional or world ranking, where would you rank against your peers?

If you were ranked 307th in the world, what could you and your coach—your director—do to get you into the top 100? The top 50? *The Top 10?*

In tennis, the strokes of the leading juniors look the same as those of the top pros. Minor differences set the two groups apart. To move up in the rankings means increased dedication and working with a coach who cajoles, inspires, and chips away at the smallest defect in each type of stroke—defects only the most practiced eyes can see.

There's no reason we can't have the same dedication to detail in magic.

Most "good" magicians are like Hershey's chocolate bars: perfectly acceptable to those who have never experienced better, but less than they could or should be. Without benchmarks, any competent performer can please a fair share of the public. But I say *that's not good enough.*

Here's another reason to raise your level. Suppose you perform for an audience of one hundred people. At the finale, sixty respond enthusiastically. I can assure you, it will appear to all—including you—that your efforts were a great success. Now suppose you make a change or two as a result of suggestions I give you, and the number of raving fans jumps modestly from sixty to seventy. Suppose also that among the ten new converts to your fan club is the decision-maker for a different, more prestigious organization. As all pros know, every show is important, because you never know what new leads might come your way. In this example, that small incremental increase in your popularity might pay off exponentially.

No performer wins the hearts of 100% of the audience, 100% of the time. But why not try?

For you, *Raise Your Level* may imply becoming better when you perform for your magic club. Or it may mean boosting your annual show-business income from the low six figures to the rarified million-dollar club.

Never settle for good enough. Sweat the details.

Raise your level.

My *Aha!* Experience

An entertainment epiphany smacked me in the face at an unlikely event: my son's bar mitzvah party. I had booked award-winning magician/mentalist Tim Conover to entertain the guests. As I stood off to the side preparing to introduce Tim, I realized this audience was unlike any other I had stood before. I knew *everyone*! I knew them well. And they knew me. Most had known me for most of my life. They knew I was a magician and mentalist and they also knew for sure that I had no special powers.

Up until that moment, audiences for me were singular: *an* audience, a single mass of strangers to be molded. This time, for the first time, singular became plural. Everywhere I looked, I saw an individual, each with his or her own history with me, and each with a specific expectation of entertainment.

Now in a few moments, Tim would be coming out to do forty-five minutes of mentalism for this assemblage of *my* uncles and aunts, *my* cousins, *my* friends, and *my* neighbors. How could poor Tim convince them he could do miraculous things?

That's when it hit me: the words that crystallized my thinking about entertainment.

They don't care.

They don't care about you, the entertainer.

They don't care about your sleights or years of practice.

They don't care about your magic awards.

They don't care about Dr. J. B. Rhine and his ESP experiments at Duke University.

They don't care about whether it's OK to mix magic and mentalism.

They don't care whether you use rare Thayer props or cheap rubber chickens.

They don't care if your tricks are original, or older than dirt.

They don't care whether you sing, manipulate coins, tell jokes, produce doves, read minds, or play Zydeco music.

My aunts and uncles, cousins, office colleagues, and neighbors didn't care what Tim Conover was about to do, and that made them exactly the same as any other audience.

They cared about themselves. They wanted to have fun. They wanted a special experience. They wanted to be moved, touched in a new way. The medium that day—mentalism—was not the message; the medium was irrelevant. Tim Conover's personality was the message, not his "tricks." The fact that his effects did in fact fry their minds happened only because of the messenger.

Put another way, I know I could have, with a couple of days' preparation, performed most of the same routines Tim did. But lacking Tim's experience with those routines, and lacking his confidence born of hundreds of successful previous performances, the performance would have faltered. My forty-five minutes would have felt like hours. His time on stage flew by. *He* was the magic, not his props.

Now, years later, I still hear compliments about his show. Until I introduced him, the audience neither knew nor cared about Tim Conover and his awards, let alone his mental miracles. He *pulled* them into his world, and from the first moments, along they went, willingly.

Too many magical performers make the Big Mistake: we think that people do actually care about the stuff I listed above.

They don't, and they won't, until they can relax because they know we're taking them on a first class journey to our world, the world of entertainment.

Say It Loud:
"I Entertain and I'm Proud!"

You are a special person. You, the entertainer.

Look at the people on the street, in the next room, at the office. Those kind souls never experience the adulation and admiration that flows over you when you successfully complete a routine. Having everyone around a table focus their attention on you, or hearing your name announced and walking out to applause, sets you apart from the multitudes who provide valuable social services and products, but not entertainment.

Non-entertainers can neither understand nor appreciate the thrill of the successfully executed moment before an audience, one which you envisioned, nurtured, hatched, and which now brings you some delicious combination of smiles, gasps, laughter, and applause.

We can luxuriate in those reactions, but behind the scenes we must work diligently to earn them, so that we can keep complacency at bay.

Look to the Stars

Every performing style can be successful, I believe, as long as certain fundamental criteria are met. You will see those criteria in the chapter on *Reactions* and *The Six Pillars of Entertainment Success*.

Lance Burton and Mac King are close friends of each other, and both are now million-dollar Las Vegas magic acts. Yet their styles could hardly be more different. Kreskin still performs in thousand-seat venues around the English-speaking world. Derren Brown, David Blaine, even Uri Geller, all present forms of what we in the business call mentalism, and again, their presentational styles vary immensely.

There must be common elements that allow each of these performers to achieve entertainment, while still maintaining his individual style. We will be examining those elements later on.

In these pages you'll see a particular focus on three performers whose work transcends the stereotypical magician or mentalist: Kreskin, David Copperfield, and David Blaine. Each has achieved that rarest level of success: his name is widely recognized by the public. Aside from their fame and financial success, they share one additional trait: derision from large segments of the magic and mentalism communities.

Now here's the interesting phenomenon. I have a small circle of friends in those communities who have risen to the top of their field. Not one of those successful performers (and in this case I measure "success" by a continual flow of repeat bookings) ever knocks Copperfield, Kreskin, or Blaine. Invariably, it's those whose careers have been stuck in neutral who scream the loudest, "Why is *he* on television?"

Before I go on, let me assure you, I do not nod approvingly and robotically at everything done by these three stars. Far from it. To name just a few issues I have with them: I look askance at the opening fifteen or twenty minutes of Kreskin's live show, which is mostly just name-dropping, and his quirky body movements. Copperfield, especially in his most recent TV specials, throws in suggestive jokes that fit neither the moment nor the persona he's built up over the years. And Blaine, well, not many of us have seen him do a live show without the miracle of editing, so I have no clue as to how successful he may be in front of a live, paying audience. Nonetheless, from time to time, we're going to examine what these three (among others) do *right*. They also suit my purposes here because they provide me with a common focal point: if you bought this book, you're likely to have seen them perform.

Kreskin, Copperfield, and Blaine: hugely successful performers of vastly differing styles. Certain common denominators allowed them to leapfrog their competition, and I've attempted to unearth those denominators for examination.

But be assured, my goal in this book is to make you the best *you*, not an imitation of me or of any particular performer whom I happen to admire.

Too Much of a Good Thing

From Singapore to Sri Lanka, from New Jersey to New South Wales, planet Earth groans under (or from) mountains of palming coins, silks, thumb tips, Hippity-Hop Rabbits and more decks of cards—marked, stripped, roughed, and smoothed—than you can shake a break-away wand at.

Yet sadly, most magic sucks.

Always has, always will. It's pure demographics.

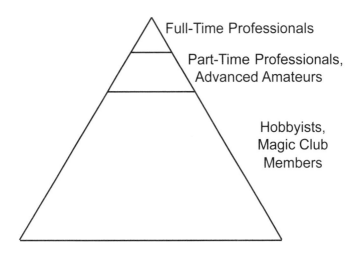

The title "full-time professional" covers a wide swath of experience and levels of success. Some "pros" earn barely enough to cover the rent, while a few top tier professionals file CEO-level tax returns.

Those in the middle tier of the pyramid also vary widely in their abilities to entertain. Some indeed possess superior technical skills, poise, and charm, and can entertain extraordinarily well.

The lucky men and women at the top of the pyramid always have the distinct advantage of being in front of audiences more often than the part-timers and the hobbyists. Nothing replaces experience. No matter how well you practice a trick for yourself, it will be different when performed for strangers. And the tenth time will usually see a marked improvement over the first time. It's been said that the amateur performs different tricks for the same people and the pro performs the same tricks for different people. And each time you perform the same trick, you grow from the experience.

All the hand wringing about the sorry state of magic is a silly exercise in futility. The above pyramid also applies to writers, musicians, painters, actors, mimes, and jugglers. And it always will. So, to those who lament the fact that so much of magic stinks, I say, get over it! Some people collect stamps fanatically for a lifetime, others do it and stop after a year. So what?

There's nothing special about magic as a pastime. If the majority of practitioners use magic as a pleasant diversion and nothing more, that's their business. They will *always* be the majority and that fact must be accepted. To the worriers, I say, worry about yourself. Each person must find his or her own level of passion and commitment.

And by the way, the fact that you are reading this book speaks directly to your sense of dedication to the art, and your desire to boost your skill level.

Competitors

What volatile college basketball coach Bobby Knight lacks in social skills, he makes up in his transcendent knowledge of his sport. In the book *A Season on the Brink*, by John Feinstein, Knight tells his players that when they are out on the basketball court, "you play against your own potential."

Got that? Not your opponents, or the refs, or even the blunders or wizardry of your teammates. You play against your own potential. It's the same for us in the entertainment game.

Every day, in every part of the developed world, tens of thousands of meetings, conferences, parties, trade shows, and other gatherings take place. Your potential to find an audience is not a function of your competitors and their programs. Your main opponent in your life as an entertainer is you—*your* potential. Master your own domain, and eventually your competitors, real or perceived, will fade from your consciousness.

If you must worry about something, worry about the mediocre among us. An inferior performer hurts you more than someone who filches a line or piece of business from your act. Bad acts, like raw garlic, linger long after the experience. A weak magician or mentalist poisons the job market for other magicians and mentalists, and the toxic effect can last for years.

Conversely, strong acts boost demand. Kreskin surely helped me and other mentalists get work in the 1970s and '80s when he was one of the most frequently booked guests on the major TV talk shows. Las Vegas didn't turn into a magic Mecca until Siegfried and Roy demolished the long-held stereotypical image of magic acts.

You have a limited amount of energy and time. Don't waste a drop of either on things beyond your control. Be the best you can be, and you'll eventually find that your only real competition is yourself.

The Dangers of Success

Many times during my years as a full-time performer, other performers made a special trip to catch my show (what greater compliment could there be?). They came because they felt they might learn something, and surely, watching others always is a wise idea, as long as you watch critically. I willingly met with fellow performers after the show and sat, Buddha-like, sharing my observations about what they had witnessed on stage.

My comments may or may not have been cogent or useful, but I now realize they lacked objectivity. Out on the road, the performer spins a cocoon around himself. The more success he achieves, the more shows he does, the more isolated from critical thinking he becomes.

He does his show and when he walks offstage, the only comments he hears are laudatory.

"You were amazing!

"We loved your show!"

"I haven't had this much fun in years!"

Unless you really screw up (set the birthday kid on fire, cut the boss's tie—for real, go thirty minutes over your allotted time), no normal person ever says an untoward word. After a few years of this, you lose the fear of failure you had early on in your career, and the urge toward introspection dissipates.

That's dangerous.

While you may be as good as they say you are, your attitude should always remain, "I'm not as good as I can be."

Personal
Entertainment
Highlights

Scattered through these chapters, I've placed a few of the moments that pop to the top of my consciousness when thinking about entertainment in our field. Not necessarily a listing of the "best," these are those few performers or performances that affected or touched me more profoundly, or more memorably, than others.

Use these observations to calibrate your vision of entertainment with mine.

A Personal Entertainment Highlight:
Al Flosso — The Miser's Dream

The diminutive man known as the Coney Island Fakir played a major role in my development as a magician. During my teen years I spent many happy Saturday afternoons in his ramshackle excuse for a magic shop, surrounded by dust, decaying props, and some of the greatest magicians in the world (although I knew none of them at the time). Sometimes Al was the kindest man in the world, giving me deep discounts and taking me and other young magicians out for a fancy New York dinner. But say the wrong word (*Tannen's*, for one), especially in front of potential paying customers, and he would launch into a ten-minute full-throated tirade.

I saw him perform his signature piece, the Miser's Dream, only once, and even though it was about forty years ago, when I was in my mid-teens, it remains indelibly etched inside my skull. He had volunteered to do a banquet benefit show for FAME (Future American Magical Entertainers), the teen-magic group to which I belonged. My mother, who had no great affection for my hobby, graciously volunteered to drive me into Manhattan and stay with me for the luncheon.

The memory I have is more than his poking around the hapless young boy from the audience, producing coins—plus various other items that should not be on a young boy—virtually non-stop. No, the memory is of my mother laughing, laughing so hard she could barely breathe, laughing and wiping away tears. I had never seen her in that state, not before, not after. A *magician* was making her laugh like that!

That day marked the beginning of her acceptance of my chosen hobby—or perhaps more accurately, the lessening of her displeasure.

Thanks, Al, for everything.

Section II

◀ PRECURSORS ▶

"Items that precede... and indicate,
suggest, or announce something to come."

Chapter 2
The Hierarchy of Mystery Entertainment

From our side of the fence, we do "effects." From the spectator's side, our routines fall into one of three broad categories:

1. **Puzzle**
2. **Trick**
3. **Extraordinary Moment**

While the lines between these categories are exceedingly blurry, most magic performed around the world falls into the first category: Puzzles. The spectator intuitively knows that what he has just seen is, to one degree or another, impossible, improbable, or just weird. He can't figure it out, but he assumes that if he knew the secret, he too could pull it off.

A *trick* is a demonstration of perceived skill, and therefore is more impressive than a puzzle. I say *perceived* skill because the audience doesn't care whether the signed card found its way into your wallet via a beautifully executed one-handed palm or one of the "no-palming-required" methods. Either way, *you* got it in there so you get credited with possessing a highly specialized and secret skill.

Overwhelmingly, professional magicians perform Tricks.

That's not a pejorative statement. Tricks have the ability to thoroughly and satisfyingly entertain. The pantheon of magic's elite thrill us—and their non-magical audiences—with Tricks.

An Extraordinary Moment leaves no room for explanation. The viewer gasps for air rather than grasp for a method. Skill is not an issue.

A perfectly executed Balducci Levitation is an Extraordinary Moment. Four Jokers that change into four Kings may elicit cries of "No freakin' way," but it's not an Extraordinary Moment; it's a terrific Trick.

A good number of the routines on David Blaine's first couple of TV specials attained Extraordinary Moment status. He literally rendered speechless many of his spectators. As magicians, we know that few of his effects required more than a moderate level of manual dexterity, yet again and again the reactions approached religious ecstasy. (I understand that we saw what the video editors wanted us to see. That's not the issue. What we *did* see was a series of extraordinary reactions.)

Mentalists, more than magicians, perform Extraordinary Moments. The particular nature of what they appear to do—delving into the minds of their audiences—engenders an intimacy with the performer that cannot be matched with demonstrations of skill, regardless of how mysterious they may be.

Close-up performers have more opportunities to deliver Extraordinary Moments than stage performers. The physical separation between the stage performer and the audience works against his achieving anything more than Tricks. Awesome, wonderful, hugely entertaining perhaps, but stage conjuring will always, with only the rare exception, fall within the Trick category.

What do you do? If you perform puzzles exceedingly well, you *can* be the life of the party. You can also make a living behind the counter at a magic shop.

People enjoy puzzles: anagrams, crossword puzzles, brainteasers. They're fun. They're also commonplace, and rarely reward the performer with a lasting career.

Superb Tricks, and the occasional Extraordinary Moment: those should be your goals.

Bona Fide Magic

What if you could perform *real* magic? You wave your hand and a cork floats up to your fingers. You rub torn pieces of paper together and they become whole again. You put three coins in your hand, close your fingers around them, and only two coins remain. You reach forward and produce a coin or a card from the air.

What if you really could do those things? Would you do them *in front of an audience*? Why?

And if you did choose to work your miracles for an audience, what would your demeanor be?

Perhaps that would depend on how difficult any particular feat was.

Would your audience become emotionally involved by watching you?

Emotions lubricate the entertainment engine, and in upcoming chapters we'll be examining techniques for boosting the emotional content of your routines.

Emotions generate real magic.

Stalking the Extraordinary Moment

The stronger the magic, the less need for "showmanship."

The typical cups and balls routine involves a cascading series of mini-climaxes. Balls appear and vanish and reappear— here, then there, then back again—all capped with a kicker ending. The best performers of this classic effect use charm and wit, along with their magic, to hold the audience's attention.

Compare that with Blaine's presentation of the Raven. A boy out on a barren lot somewhere in Middle America... a coin on his hand is there... David waves his hand over the coin, and the coin is not there. Vanished! The boy stands, transfixed, perplexed. After a long moment, he softly mutters, while still staring at his hand, "Cool."

Between the best cups and balls routine and Blaine's Raven, which will be remembered a week later? The spectators at the Magic Castle enjoyed the balls mystifyingly coming and going— that is, the tricks—while that scruffy kid had an Extraordinary Moment: *a coin disappeared from his hand!* No props, no "moves" that he was aware of, not one word of useless patter.

Warning: Do not take this as invitation to copy Blaine's style. His laconic, half-stoned persona probably fits you like a cheap suit on a humid day. I just want to point out that Extraordinary

41

Moments can be brought forth from props and effects you already own.

It's *you* who makes the moment trivial.

It's *you* who can make the moment extraordinary.

Magic for Magicians vs. Magic for Everyone Else

When you read a magic book or magazine, if the description of the "effect" goes on for more than a couple of sentences, it's probably best done for other magicians. Laypeople want direct plots. Anything else is magical masturbation, done because it makes you feel good, and no one else.

What do people remember? It's easy to find out—just ask someone who recently saw a magician or mentalist to tell you what they saw. You'll hear responses similar to these:

"This guy put a nickel and dime in my hand and when I opened my hand the dime disappeared."

"He had this girl look at a word in a book and he told her the word she was thinking about."

"I picked a card and

... he told me what it was."

... it jumped into his pocket."

... he tore it up and put it back together."

"Siegfried put Roy in a box and covered it for a second and then Roy was gone and a tiger was there!"

"He floated!"

Take a look at a magic book or magazine and see how many effects could be described that succinctly. Typically, you see card tricks that involve red cards from blue back decks, counting, weak climaxes, and convoluted plots that force the audience to follow the action closely.

That's magic for us and our buddies. It won't get you repeat gigs.

Consider this excerpt from an interview with David Blaine that appeared in *Newsday*, the Long Island, New York newspaper, on November 7, 2002. Reporter David Behrens wrote the story, and the interview took place in Blaine's New York City apartment.

[Blaine] produces a fresh, unopened deck of cards.

When the deck is thoroughly shuffled, he fans the cards and asks one of his visitors: "Think of a card."

He places the deck on the arm of a chair and he will not touch the deck again. The visitor is instructed to pick up the deck, hold it in his left hand and announce which card he selected.

"The three of hearts," the visitor says.

"Now cut the deck somewhere in the middle," Blaine says. The deck is cut and the top half of the cards set aside.

"That's your card," Blaine says, indicating the top card on the lower half of the deck.

The visitors are silent, astonished.

The card, naturally, is the three of hearts.

Now, first fight the urge to analyze the "how" of the effect. Newspaper reporters are no better than others at accurately remembering all the details of a trick, so this may not be exactly what transpired.

The important issue here is that, as in most of Blaine's magic, overt "show business" never makes an appearance, and the plot—think of a card, cut the cards, that's your card—could not be more to the point. The spectators had an Extraordinary Moment. They sat "silent, astonished."

The stronger the magic, the less need for showmanship. The corollary, naturally, must be that weaker magic requires more help from the performer, and that's where lack of natural talent rears its ugly head. If you're not an extroverted or dramatic person in real life, you especially need to raise your showmanship level for your less powerful effects. (You'll learn how later on.)

Most performed magic is weak, and most magic sold in magic shops or written about in the magic periodicals is best performed only for others interested in the art.

The best performed magic and mentalism have always been, and always will be, direct, immediately understandable, and compelling enough to be recalled days later.

How much of your show fits that description?

The Trivialization of Magic

Routines tumble down the above hierarchy (i.e., Extraordinary Moments become Tricks, and Tricks become Puzzles) because of the attitude of the performer. When he treats a trick—or any magical moment—as easy, commonplace, or anything other than special, he dulls the impact of that routine. A trivial stunt by definition cannot be special, yet we see this attitude every day in magic.

A specific example: On the Website for L&L Publishing (llpub.com) I came across a video clip from one of the most respected performers and teachers in magic, Michael Ammar. The Website blurb said: "Michael Ammar does the impossible as he performs 'The Floating Lifesaver' in this clip from 'Easy To Master Thread Miracles' Volume 3."

Here's what we see: Michael, standing in front of the usual L&L audience of excessively enthusiastic and good-looking young adults, starts by saying,

You know, when I was growing up, my favorite candy was a Lifesaver, you know…and I used to eat these little things and think 'Why are these 'life savers'?' I mean, 'cause as a kid I'm just like, well, these must, like, save people's lives, and I didn't realize it was like this little thing that you would throw overboard and everything. But Lifesavers to me always represented this really amazing, uhhh, possibility, you know, so I thought I'd do something with a Lifesaver.

Now let's see, I'm gonna see if I can't get it trained here… let's see…

And he whistles at the Lifesaver as if it were a cute pet and, sure enough, it moves, then floats around in front of him and finally it floats all the way up into his mouth.

After the candy floats up to his mouth, he laughs along with the spectators, and says, "Isn't that neat?"

Now, lest you misunderstand my comments, this is *a brilliant and baffling effect.* (And my guess is that Michael does not perform in this manner for paid gigs.) The candy truly floats around in wonderfully mysterious ways.

But what's with the patter? It's not especially funny; it doesn't tell the audience anything fascinating or clever or interesting. Instead, it almost mocks the magic itself by momentarily shifting the focus to the young Michael and his sweet tooth and his questions about candy. Then the hackneyed ploy of whistling at an object before it moves, which may play fine at children's shows, but serves little purpose when presented to adults.

"But Lifesavers to me always represented this really amazing, uhhh, possibility, you know, so I thought I'd do something with a Lifesaver."

Why did they represent an amazing possibility? It's a non-sequitur that is suddenly thrown into the patter.

"So I thought I'd do something with a Lifesaver."

"Do something"? It sounds so casual. Not mysterious, not funny, not dramatic, it's the type of remark that might be said by an interior decorator—"let's puhleeeeze do something with that window treatment!"—but it's not terribly appropriate for a miracle worker.

Again, this trick is a piece of strong magic. It's the presentation that squelches a potential Extraordinary Moment into a very nice Trick.

Think about every word you say. Analyze your every action. This is *not* a quick process. I watched that brief clip many times before I began to appreciate its strengths and the potential areas for improvement.

You want your presentational skills to equal or exceed your magic technique. Both goals require time, dedication, and effort.

All magic, at its core, is a Puzzle. Presentation—and presentation only—is the lever that elevates a Puzzle to a Trick, or a Trick to an Extraordinary Moment.

Raise your level.

Chapter 3

Reactions

There is only one purpose for doing *anything* in front of an audience: *to get a reaction.*

Whether you're a singer, comedian, musician, poet, or magician, if they stare blankly back at you, you failed. Doing something for your own pleasure may qualify you as an artist, but recognize that the entertainer *requires* specific audience reactions.

So the question becomes: *What reactions do you want?*

What reaction do you want for the trick as a whole?

What reaction do you want for each moment within the routine?

You have not completed your work on a routine until you answer those questions.

The Big Three

As performers of mystical entertainment, the reactions we most value are:

1. **Rapt Attention**
2. **Laughter**
3. **Astonishment**

(Applause, another form of reaction, may follow any of the above.)

Ideally, *every* moment leads to one of these reactions.

And anything that fails to deliver a sought-after reaction is *filler!*

All performances have filler material. Sometimes it's the necessary explanations about why you're about to do what you do, or it may be the instructions needed to accomplish the trick. Other times it's the transition from moment to moment, or from trick to trick.

Regardless of the type of filler, it's an absolute fact that successful performers reduce such material to its absolute minimum.

To put it another way, if I'm not enthralled, amused, or amazed by your words or your actions—and I mean *every word* and *every action*—I'm on my way to being bored, and Entertainment will shortly be leaving the building.

In subsequent pages you'll read about specific instances of well-known performers inserting useless, off-target filler into their routines. We all do it. But with a disciplined approach to our scripting and performing, we can nip and tuck our way to leaner, tighter routines.

When I talk about "necessary instructions", I mean phrases such as:

- "Please remove a card from the deck."
- "Step over here and examine these three rings."
- "Say 'Stop' as I flip though the pages."

Necessary explanations:

- "Scientists use these strange symbols to test for extrasensory perception."
- "The envelope hanging from the ceiling has been securely sealed and in full view from the time I began."
- "This is a Samurai sword, used by nimble warriors in ancient Japan to slay enemies and open envelopes."

When you write out your Script (see the chapter on *Scripting and Rehearsing*), and when you watch yourself on tape, rigorously assess which words and—equally important—which actions are needless filler. Separate those filler words and actions from the words and actions that progressively drive you toward your desired reactions.

The best magicians and mentalists continually weave their audiences through the Big Three reactions. They seamlessly move from Laughter to Rapt Attention and then on to the climax, the moment of Astonishment.

The broadest category of the Big Three Reactions is Rapt Attention. It's easy to know if you've hit this target: just look at the audience. Are they deeply engaged in your words or actions? If you don't have the full attention of all, you've missed this target.

You can walk down many paths on your way to achieving the Rapt Attention reaction. Your words may be:

- Dramatic
- Charming
- Heartwarming
- Fascinating/Interesting
  - Engrossing Stories, especially those of a personal nature
  - Unusual or Useful Information
    - "Strange but true."
    - "Here's how card sharks cheat you."

Sell the Sizzle, Not the Steak.

People react to people. We respond when we see another person's emotions.

David Blaine's TV specials showed us—the viewers—the reactions of his audiences (sometimes an audience of one). Blaine and his associates snubbed the usual TV-magic-special focus on the performer and his skills. Instead, they allowed us to bask in the gleeful and often awestruck reactions of those who witnessed his feats. More than anything else, it was this single decision by Blaine's creative team—focusing on the reaction more than the trick—that catapulted his specials into the ratings stratosphere.

Magicians often fail to grasp the value of reactions and they make one of two major mistakes:

1. They don't allow the reaction to fully develop. They move too quickly to the next moment of the routine.
2. They don't put the reactor in a position where others in the audience can see and hear the reaction.

Mentalists especially fall victim to this syndrome: they talk to people who remain seated in the audience. The performer can see the look of astonishment, but few others can. Much better to have the person stand. That way the rest of the audience can share the excitement of the moment.

People relate to people. We laugh when others laugh, we cry communally, we feel the embarrassment of a volunteer's awkward moment on stage, we empathize greatly with people we know, and only somewhat less so with strangers. Again, the team behind the Blaine TV specials understood this. Magicians watched the first special and saw Blaine perform a double lift and a top change, and then they exclaimed about how they could do it better. What did the rest of the world see? Something brief about two cards changing places—but mostly they saw a locker room full of Dallas Cowboy pro football players recoiling from what they saw and then laughing and slapping each other in a moment of great and shared joy. On screen, the reaction lasted far longer than the trick.

The entire show followed that format, and the high audience ratings lead to reruns and further TV specials. Actions and decisions that had magicians scratching their collective heads, delighted the public.

The Blaine team sold the sizzle, not the steak. That works in advertising, and you ought to let that adage guide you as you polish your performances.

Whenever possible, sell the reaction, not the trick.

Fizzle vs. Sizzle

In early 2003, I attended a public performance of a preeminent writer and theorist about all things magical. His forty-minute set consisted exclusively of card tricks, and during that time I looked to my left and to my right and in just my one row I saw several people sleeping! And I saw others in the audience nodding off as well. This state of affairs sets off a chain reaction, as it becomes clear to all that audience reaction is increasingly subdued. I've since been told that what I witnessed in the audience that night was, sadly, not an uncommon occurrence for this technically skilled and rather famous (to us) name in magic.

What went wrong? First, much of his show was set up as an implicit challenge—I will fool you and you won't be able to catch me—but few in the audience cared to take the challenge. In the upcoming chapter on the Six Pillars of Entertainment Success, you'll read about the need to Communicate Your Humanity. He didn't, and the audience reacted with chilly indifference.

Then too, I wondered, what's the point of his show? Rather than homing in on the above Big Three Reactions, the subtext of his show seemed to be:

I can do things with playing cards that you can't. Here, let me prove it to you. Now let me prove it to you again. One more time, but slightly differently. Still not convinced? Then I'll prove it to you ten or twenty more times.

Zzzzzz...

Here's a performer who has mastered the *technique* of magic, but not the *Magic* of magic. And of course, he's a typical specimen on the magic scene.

One might say that his target reaction was Astonishment. He certainly achieved astonishment from time to time. But his forty-minute set, taken as a whole experience, failed to achieve solid Entertainment for too many of those minutes.

His setup for each trick rarely targeted either Laughter or Rapt Attention. That is, when explaining what he was doing, or about to do, he was infrequently funny, and almost never Heartwarming, Fascinating, Dramatic, Charming, or anything else that pulled the audience into his world. Personal involvement came into play only for the few spectators who joined him on stage.

His filler material overwhelmed the desired reactions of his words and physical actions. In the following chapters, we'll examine what he, and you, can and should do to avoid the problems he created for himself.

Instead of demonstrating "effects," let's make Magic.

Chapter 4
The Six Pillars of Entertainment Success

Psst. Hey, magician guy. You like secrets, don't you? You want secrets? I got 'em. You are about to read the true and eternal secrets of entertainment success.

OK, they're not "trick" secrets. These are the secrets that count, that separate the wannabes from the arrived. These are the steadfast secrets that no masked magician can expose, for the true performance secrets are just that, secrets of theatrical *performance,* and not the flimsy methodology of mere deception.

Here is your roadmap, your can't-fail guide to success as an entertainer. Use these pillars to take the measure of your act.

These Pillars revealed themselves after hundreds of hours of analyzing the work of performers at the top skill levels, and—specifically—asking why *this* particular routine is successful. And why other routines, sometimes offered by those same performers, fall short.

Nebulous at first, the keys to entertainment success gelled into six supernovas, and that's what you'll find below. *All* successful entertainment in our field is built upon these pillars. As you view videos of yourself and become your own director, let these tenets help you raise your level.

As mystery entertainers, it is not enough for us to fool people. There must be more. The "more" is entertainment, and I want you to achieve maximum entertainment.

Toward that end, I present to you the real secrets of the Real Work:

1. **Master Your Craft**

2. **Communicate Your Humanity**

3. **Capture the Excitement**

4. **Control Every Moment**

5. **Eliminate Weak Spots**

6. **Build to a Climax**

1. Master Your Craft

Once, back when I was a newly hatched professional entertainer, a much older, fairly well-established magician came to see me perform. After the show, he laid a few nice compliments on me and then, seeking to pass on some wisdom from experience, he told me, "Remember, it's not *what* you do, it's *how* you do it."

Well, yes. And no.

What he meant—and many others have said or written similar sentiments—was that the presentation of a trick overrides the trick itself. That's true, assuming you execute the trick perfectly. *Lacking technical proficiency, all else fails.* That applies to any artist, but as mystery workers we have an added technical hurdle to surmount: the audience must be fooled. They cannot be aware of the "secret something."

Even those magicians whose acts revolve around "failure" (Ballantine being the best known) still must perfectly master the timing and intricacies of their performance.

I hope you don't need this book to motivate you to practice, practice, practice. Diligently practice your moves until they flow effortlessly and automatically. Then set about the job of rehearsing your stage movements and your lines. Master your script. When you're in front of strangers, the last thing you want to worry about is what to say or do next. Every word must be the right word at the right moment.

You practice the moves first. Then you rehearse the routine. Then you rehearse the entire act, start to finish. If you rehearse in disjointed pieces, you don't capture the flow of the act, and you run the risk of not noticing that certain moments don't flow smoothly into the next. Even supposedly simple things, such as opening a card box and later replacing the cards, require practice so you don't fumble around. And for just about every magician it is important that you do your final rehearsals in the clothes you will be wearing. You don't want to be on stage when you discover that the pocket you need isn't in this suit.

Study the videos of yourself. Make sure you see yourself from different angles, and during different shows. Most laypeople, especially in close-up situations, are too nice to tell you they saw something they shouldn't have. A coin that flashes at the wrong moment, a hand held awkwardly when a card is palmed, an untimely glance at a hidden billet, a dead bird plopping to the floor (OK, you would notice that one), all work to deduct points from the imaginary scorecards your audiences hold in their heads.

One hesitates to quantify this issue, but it seems to me that perhaps 80%–90% of all problems magicians encounter relate directly to their lack of intense and proper preparation. So I'm assuming you've put in the requisite hours perfecting the technical aspects of your performance. If not, all else in this book will be for naught.

Man and Superman

Nothing in show business comes easily. It takes hard work to look as if you're not working at all. Looking natural on stage is an unnatural act. If you let nature take its course, when you walk out in front of strangers your pants would be moist in inappropriate places. So you put in the hours of practice to walk out with your head up and shoulders back, confident in your skills and in your knowledge of your material.

Master your specialty—cards, coins, mentalism, escapes, whatever—and then be certain you choose the strongest material you can confidently perform.

In my lectures, I frequently talk about the entertainer as Superman, for I believe that's a useful analogy. During most of the day, that caped super-hero strolls among the populace of Metropolis appearing to all as nothing more than a mild-mannered reporter. A regular guy. Then, at the appropriate moment, he becomes a better version of himself. Ever Clark Kent at his core, when called upon to perform, he nonetheless demonstrates extraordinary abilities.

As entertainers, we all possess extraordinary abilities—skills and talents that other people lack. If we didn't, there would be no reason to watch us.

Thinking of yourself as a version of Superman is a helpful exercise. You may be a humble Superman, or a flamboyant one; you may be a fast-talking Superman from a great metropolitan city, or you may have a down-home drawl, but one thing you will be is confident. Sure of yourself, and secure in your abilities.

You want to be similar to the folks down front, but with a few special attributes and skills that flow effortlessly from you.

That's why you must practice thoroughly, if not compulsively. People don't want to see *themselves* on stage, at least not ordinary versions of themselves. They want to see Superman. They want to believe in the *potential* of a Superman. The more thoroughly prepared you are, the easier it becomes to project an air of invincibility.

Also, you can be most relaxed when you can turn on your internal cruise control; only then can you steer your act to unexplored territory. Only then can you confidently interact spontaneously with your audiences.

Work at your craft. Make yourself invincible.

In the chapter on Choosing Material, we'll look at how to narrow down your choices to the best tricks for you. Once you find them, practice them diligently.

Strive to do a few things extraordinarily well. Most magicians do an extraordinary number of things poorly. Achieving your own level of artistic integrity requires fluency of technique, for only then will you be free to express originality. And the degree of fluency, of technical mastery, is inextricably linked to the time and effort spent in practicing moves and rehearsing the full routine.

This is not a handbook of conjuring technique. For that you will embrace the best of magic's volumes, videos, lecturers, teachers, and mentors. From them you will learn how to misdirect, how to "change the moment," how to perform jazz magic and mentalism everywhere and anywhere. As I said earlier, use this book for the "everything else."

And practice it all—performance technique and trick technique—with care and passion.

The Road Less Traveled

As a final comment on Mastering Your Craft, let me share a thought from Bob Cassidy's for-mentalists-only Website. In this excerpt he examines the merits of using a deck stack that requires a quick calculation versus using mnemonics to memorize the position of every card:

"But the calculation is easy," you might reply. And it may well be "easy." The problem is that the calculation may suddenly become very difficult if you try to do it while interacting with the audience. Of course, you can just stand there and stare up in the air for a second while everyone wonders if you are having a stroke, thus adding some unexpected drama to your act.

Or you can come to the realization that the hard way is actually the easy way. And besides, the calculation stack is a one-trick pony. When you learn [how] to memorize a deck of cards you automatically learn to memorize just about anything else.

Now disregard, momentarily at least, the calculation vs. mnemonics argument (they both have substantial merit). Did one line jump out at you? One sentence stopped me cold:

Or you can come to the realization that the hard way is actually the easy way.

That brilliant insight applies to life and entertainment. The easy way leads to short-term gains but rarely long-term success.

The successful performers of my acquaintance consciously and conscientiously take the hard way, for that will be what separates them from the herd. They are not frightened by solitary hours of study and development, followed by years of practice and rehearsal. Rather, they thrive on it. They understand that seeking the easy way is the path taken by the majority. And if you are buried among the majority, consigned to mediocrity, or worse, *accepting mediocrity*, you can never be exceptional.

The hard way becomes the easy way as distractions evaporate in the heat of self-imposed focus.

And the easy way, the frittering from one trick to the next before mastery is achieved, becomes hard as it continually leads to false starts and unfulfilled expectations.

Which path will you take?

2. Communicate Your Humanity

Work to establish rapport with your audience immediately.

You are a stranger to them, and their moms told them to be wary of strangers. Let them know that "we're in this together," and together we're going to transcend your workaday lives. Once you manage to build a strong, empathetic bond with your audience, you can make the dumbest mistakes, crazy external foul-ups can befall you, and your audience will still be on your side, *wanting* to see you succeed!

The likeable performer always performs with a sterling advantage: an extra level of goodwill. Heckler-stopper lines become unnecessary because, without prompting from you, audience members themselves will shush the uninvited participants.

Woe to the performer who fails to build rapport with the folks out front. For him the audience will exit mentally, if not physically, at the first sign of weakness. This applies equally to all entertainers.

Here's what *New York Times* theater critic Alessandra Stanley had to say in her May 6, 2003 review of comedian Bill Maher's Broadway show:

Mr. Maher is clever and provocative, but he is no Oscar Wilde. Behind his riffs there is a self-righteous tone that makes him hard to like... And a successful live performance usually requires a secret lovability.

A secret lovability. A performer may project a gruff exterior, yet if somehow the audience feels a human connection, they look past the outer layer. (Consider the success of insult-comedian Don Rickles.)

Further on, Ms. Stanley writes:

[Maher's] body language is defiant, not welcoming.

It's all part of a total package: your words, your body language, your attitude. This advice has passed from Nate Leipzig to Dai Vernon to all: *If they like you, they will like what you do.* It's certainly true, now and forever, that a charismatic person in politics, sales, or show business starts with a leg up on the competition. In this section, we'll look at the things you can do to boost your likability quotient.

That said, however, I also believe that communicating your humanity, exposing who you are as a person, supersedes—or at least precedes—likability. We empathize with many a movie villain (Michael Corleone of the Godfather films is one classic example), but we never "like" them. In either case—hero or villain—the entertainment score ratchets up when we connect, on a human level, with the person we're watching.

*   *   *

How do you communicate humanity? Here are several techniques:

a) Give 'em a smile.

Smiles, the first and easiest way to communicate humanity, require no rehearsal and cost nothing, so fling them about with abandon. A smile says you feel comfortable being in front of us; it radiates confidence and friendliness. An unsmiling performer had better have an excellent reason for the look on his face, because he's not communicating his connection with the audience members, and he'll be seen as cold and standoffish.

59

A sincere smile transcends language, age, race, and cultural differences. It's the universally understood message of friendliness, of "I'm happy to be here, with *you*."

Here's a trick I use: Just before I walk out on stage I say something funny to someone backstage. Actually, it's not always truly funny; it may be just silly or friendly. The words don't matter. The goal is to put a smile on *my* face; that's the face I want the audience to see first. I don't want to expose my nervousness or preoccupation with the new bit I'm still developing. Using this smile "trick" not only places the look I want upon my countenance, it also helps relax me. There's likely a good physiological reason for it, but smiling sends a calming message to the rest of my body.

It will for you too.

b) Tell 'em a story.

David Copperfield, amidst all the trappings of a weighty mega stage show, tells stories (some of which, I'm sorry to tell you, may not be completely true!) about growing up, about his family, and sometimes about his fears. If he didn't do that, he'd be subsumed, as are so many other illusionists, by his own props, dancers, glitter, and music, and we'd have no sense of who this guy is.

You and others in our field may have tired of his borderline sappy narratives, but I would rather see him take that risk than see him mask himself behind the music and the scenery and the dancers and the tricks. Copperfield understands that illusionists especially must strive to communicate a human personality, lest they become nothing more than animated props in their own shows.

But as with anything else, there are stories and there are stories. Every story you tell must have as its goal one of the Big Three Reactions. A story becomes counterproductive if it meanders or fails to communicate something significant.

Edit your stories the way a writer would, scrutinizing each word, questioning whether it hits a specific, targeted reaction. Consider with care where you are headed. Into which category do your words fall? Funny? Sad? Fascinating? Anecdotes from your life humanize you, but be certain that they have impact.

c) Acknowledge your surroundings.

At the very least, a few early words along the lines of, "It's nice to be here in the beautiful town of Detroit Vista Hills," or "Thanks for inviting me to be part of the Who's-Your-Daddy Sales and Marketing Roundup," sends the message that you're doing more than pressing "Play" on your mental tape recorder.

If appropriate, consider mentioning the physical environment.

"What amazing portraits! Are any of those folks here tonight?"

"I know it's a bit cool in the tent today, but together we're going to heat this joint up!"

d) React and respond.

During the show, look for opportunities to signal that "I'm here for *you.* I'm here *today*, doing this show, which is different from any other show I have ever done or will do."

Stuff happens. Use it to your benefit.

If everyone hears a loud noise during your show and you ignore it, you seem artificial, removed from the reality of the moment. If a waiter trips, a light explodes, a backdrop drops, acknowledge it in some way. Your reaction might be quick and superficial, but any reaction usually is better than none. Yes, sometimes you will be at a moment in the show when any deviation from your usual script will detract from the effect. Those moments are fewer than you imagine, and you will need to make that decision on a case-by-case basis. In most situations, you will be better served by turning the disruption into an advantage. (No one mastered this better than Uri Geller. No matter what happens, he apologizes for it, implying that once in a while his "powers" just get away from him!)

On the other hand, a sneeze in the audience, a coughing spell, people rudely talking—these are examples of distractions that usually affect the performer more than the audience as a whole, and in most cases you're better served by *not* disrupting the 'flow of your show. I've seen too many performers stop and comment on something that I barely perceived.

Kreskin, for one, knows the difference. I read a report that when he was briefly heckled during one of his full-evening performances he lowered his handheld microphone (so that only a few in the room would hear him) and said something directly to the heckler. He then continued with his story as if nothing had happened. He handled the situation without disrupting the flow and without ceding any control to the heckler. Most of the audience had no idea that anything had transpired.

The rule of thumb here is to acknowledge only those noises or incidents that are seen or heard by at least half the audience.

e)   Reveal your humanity with emotions.

In my college acting classes, we were continually urged to "stay in the moment." The actor, internally, must experience what he seeks to project externally. All successful performing artists must do the same. If we want to project surprise, we must *feel* surprised. Similarly for wonder, frustration ("That *wasn't* your card?"), glee, trepidation, and so on.

Do you feign interest in your act, moment by moment? Or do you truly feel, within your core, the emotions inherent in your words and actions? Robert-Houdin's words from the dusty past remain true: we are actors playing the role of [real] magicians. An acting class or two, along with reading up on acting technique, will surely enhance your ability to communicate your feelings.

When I was in high school I was the youngest member of a community theater group. That experience exposed me for the first time to the techniques of the theatrical director, and it forced me to understand that one cannot simply read lines and move around the stage, avoiding bumping into the scenery and other players. Acting requires significant mental preparation and physical rehearsal, more than non-actors realize. The ability to reveal emotions, *true* emotions, is an ability lacking in too many magicians.

You need to reveal a part of who you are, and you do that by letting us glimpse your innards, your emotions. Acting classes and involvement in theatrical productions help achieve that goal.

You can also *reveal your humanity with emotions* by sharing that which stirs you.

Siegfried and Roy continually talk about the "magic and mystery... of *life*." They work hard to show us, amidst their glittering production numbers, who they are as people, what their individual passions are, and that allows their show to become much more than simply about the magic. They want you to feel you have glimpsed the two stars as separate human beings. You grasp Siegfried's thrill in overcoming the impossible, and you viscerally appreciate Roy's love for the animals in the show.

Is there something in your act that relates to an emotion, a passion in your life? Can you figure out a way to share it? In Doug Henning's case, he brilliantly communicated his passion for the magic itself! Performers who expose something of their inner being, who share more than a series of tricks and jokes, connect with audiences far more strongly than those who don't.

f) Maintain eye contact.

Think about your own experiences in an audience. When the performer looks directly at you, you feel drawn into the show more strongly than you were just moments before. Eye contact is universal; we all succumb to its power and we all feel snubbed when we don't get it. As an audience member, I understand that you cannot gaze solely at me, but I also want you to look in my direction now and then.

The basic guidelines for eye contact are:

• Try never to utter one word unless you are looking at a pair of eyes.

• Don't lock on any one person for more than a second or two, unless you have a specific reason to do so.

• Don't mumble anything while looking at your props; talk to people, not things.

Certified 100% Natural

The late Marcello Truzzi—magician, raconteur, respected university scholar and researcher, and great friend of the Psychic Entertainers Association—told me this story:

> *A guy goes into an agent's office with an elephant. "Have I got an act for you! This elephant does the greatest act you'll ever see!"*
>
> *"Yeah, that's what they all say. What's he do?"*
>
> *"Impressions... best you've ever seen." And sure enough, the pachyderm does James Cagney and Cary Grant and Jimmy Stewart and on and on. And they're all pretty good.*
>
> *"So whaddya think?" says the anxious owner.*
>
> *The agent says, "Lemme talk to the elephant... alone." When the owner leaves the room the agent walks up to the side of the elephant, tenderly puts his arm way up on the elephants neck and quietly says into his great big floppy ear, "Kid, I like ya', but I got two words of advice... Be yourself!"*

Trust me, when Marcello told the story it was hilarious, but whether reading it on paper made you smile or not, the lesson holds true.

Artificiality in front of an audience rarely pays off, yet one of the most common mistakes we see is the performer who acts unnaturally. He or she tries too hard to ingratiate, or to appear dramatic, funny, or clever. Movements become exaggerated, speech patterns sound artificial, and the audience quickly picks up on it.

You Communicate Your Humanity by *being yourself.* With rare exceptions, the most successful performers present *themselves* on stage—polished, confident versions of their off-stage selves.

Often this move away from naturalness begins as an attempt—conscious or otherwise—to mimic another performer. Thus, when Kreskin was appearing on all the TV talk shows, young mentalists aped his routines and, far worse, his sometimes mangled speech patterns. Copperfield inspired legions of smoldering, love-sick-puppy magicians. And now we see the David Blaine knock-offs, accosting innocent park-dwellers and street people with, "Wanna see something cool?"

I saw a stark, real-life example of this common failing at a magic convention in 2003. The performer in question, a young full-time professional, did what I would rate as an "adequate" twenty-minute stage show. But the following morning, during his lecture, his real self showed up—and it was an instantly recognizable improvement!

This performer had layered his stage act with patent artificiality; he postured and preened and feigned involvement with the mystery and magic. His act was no better or worse than we typically see at conventions and it was reasonably well received by a majority of the audience.

During the lecture, however, he relaxed. Gone were the "stage movements" and hyperactive oomph from the night before. He just talked, with no obvious I-am-in-my-entertainer-mode theatrics. Instead, now he spoke to us with sincere passion about his particular specialty. He shared some brilliant insights and he glowed in the enthusiastic response he received from the lecture attendees. And when he brought a woman up on stage to participate in the demonstration, he treated her warmly and with charm; the previous night he pushed and shoved and ordered his volunteers around.

I would not have given much more thought to his act had I not seen the lecture. But the contrast between the two "performances" was a bit of a shock, and it served as a great lesson. When we in the lecture audience had a chance to see the real "man behind the curtain," we saw unadulterated talent, and even better, we saw an immensely likeable human being with whom we could connect. His challenge, and yours, is to blast away everything that puts up a wall between those of us in your audience, and the best qualities of your inner being, your polished version of yourself.

Looking again at Kreskin, Copperfield, and Blaine... when you see them being interviewed on talk shows, especially the more informal ones, what you see are personalities remarkably similar to the ones you see when they are performing their practiced routines. And I believe that to be a major factor in the phenomenal success they have each achieved.

The exception to this, of course, is the performer playing a character. In that case, you have to Communicate the Humanity of *that* character and you must do it by staying solidly faithful to the personality and traits of that character. You cannot go back and forth between your "normal" personality and, say, a riverboat gambler, a clown, or as in the case of Cardini's iconic act, a slightly inebriated aristocrat.

Overwhelmingly, however, magicians and mentalists play *themselves* as they demonstrate amazing things, and for them, the strong advice to "be yourself" applies.

All theater is based on *something* artificial. Our task as mystery workers is to present only the *necessary* artificial moments, and to hang those moments on the most natural framework.

Say, Young Fella, Ain't You One of Us?

An observation here about Max Maven: In the 1970s and '80s I expected Max to overtake and replace Kreskin as the leading mentalist in America. He had (and still has) all the tools—a vast and deep knowledge of magic and mentalism, a solid grounding in theatrical technique, and an abiding passion for the art form. Yet he never had the breakthrough *with the public* that I thought was his for the taking (although he—and alter-ego Phil Goldstein—did rise, and deservedly so, to the top ranks within the magic community). Max Maven, as a mentalist performing before a lay audience having no idea who this guy is, fulfilled all the Pillars of Entertainment Success, except this one. Instead of communicating his humanity, he explicitly conveyed his separateness from the rest of us.

With his Dracula-reminiscent makeup and a haughty, sometimes demeaning bearing, he sends out a message that he is *not* one of us, not a standard-issue man who happened to develop a few extraordinary skills. Instead, he stands aloof, apart. And, over the long run, I believe, it worked against him.

Magician Criss Angel also wears darkly sinister makeup. Yet he frequently plays against the Goth image we first encounter, so that by the time his show concludes we do feel that we have been watching a likeable, very human young man.

Or consider Marc Salem, arguably the most successful mentalist of the past decade. His "Mind Games" show has been a smash hit, with extended runs in, among other places, New York, London, Toronto, Montreal, Edinburgh, Melbourne, and Sydney. The reviews (not from magic publications but from the mainline theatrical press) ranged from "very good" to "you've-got-to-see-this-guy!" raves. In many of these reviews, the writer took space to elaborate on Marc's rapport with the audience, his friendly, approachable manner, along with his ability to wrest laughs from just about anything thrown his way. While his technique as a mentalist is flawless, clearly it's his humanity that wins him fans among those most difficult to please: professional theater critics.

The bottom line here is that choosing to play a character is fine, as long as it doesn't hide your humanity and thus work against your ultimate goal of entertaining your audience.

Your Audience Wants You.

You have secrets that have nothing to do with magic or mentalism; they are the secrets that make you... *you.* That make you unique. Anyone can show me a trick with a prop, but only you can inject a scintilla of your life history into that trick. You start your program as a blank slate. At the conclusion of your performance, do we know the *person* manipulating the props?

Reveal yourself. But make it real. An audience senses pretense the way a dog sniffs contraband; it's a natural ability heightened by experience.

A fuller vision of you will always be a more interesting vision than that blank slate.

To sum up this section, you Communicate Your Humanity by answering the question, "Who Are You?"

Tell me, show me.

Only then can I trust you to take me into your world.

3. Capture the Excitement

Incredible but true, too many magicians forget or overlook the beating heart of the conjuring art.

That's why in this section I ask you, *What's special?*

What's special about *this* trick? What's special about the climax of this routine? Often, magicians whiz right through the key elements of the routine, and the audience is more perplexed than entertained.

Milbourne Christopher, noted magical historian and prolific author, knew everything about magic—except how to present it. In its October 2002 issue, *Genii* ran a review of a video tape, *The Milbourne Christopher Memorial: Volume 1*. Here's an excerpt from that column, written by Joe M. Turner:

> *Another quick sequence follows in which Mr. Christopher follows the old style of performing trick after trick after trick in almost blinding speed. A flash of fire and a cane becomes two silks. The silks are transformed into a Botania... The billiard ball manipulations and productions are so fast that you barely have time to figure out what he's doing before he's on to the next trick, catching birds in a net. The birds are promptly vanished in a Tear-Away box and a lady jumps out of a Doll House to finish the sequence.*

We've all seen acts like that. And acts like that are why, for decades, magic stayed firmly affixed to the bottom rung of the show business ladder.

What's special within his act?

A blur of great magic is still just a blur. The act described above was a blur of weak magic (or strong magic made weak); Christopher was influenced by his predecessors and he in turn was emulated by thousands.

What is the essence of our art of magic? It's the excitement of doing impossible things.

You must show that excitement to your audience.

If you hold a billiard ball in your otherwise empty hand, it is impossible for another ball to suddenly appear. Absolutely, by the commonly accepted laws of nature, impossible. If you, by some unknown means cause a second ball to materialize, that's miraculous. An observer should be thinking, "It can't be! You made something from nothing! This is the most amazing thing I've ever seen!"

But wait. Now there's a third ball. And a fourth. And now they're changing color. And now there are only three again. And now there are eight. I guess what I thought was impossible is possible. In fact, look at those balls come and go... it must be easy. I don't know how it's happening, but it sure seems easy for him.

"The billiard ball manipulations and productions are so fast that you barely have time to figure out what he's doing before he's on to the next trick..."

A blur. Nothing memorable. And nothing will be remembered a day later.

Capture the excitement. Show me the difficulty. Explain, in words or gestures, why the magic part of your trick is *magic.* Not a puzzle, not a science experiment, not juggling, but *magic.*

Do you throw away the strong moments of your act? You may, because the strong moments have become mundane to you. After years of hanging around other magicians, after having performed your favorite tricks hundreds of times, it's understandable that *you* may no longer see the *magic* in your act.

Fight that tendency.

Look at Kreskin, Copperfield, and Blaine. *Everything* they do is special.

They rarely toss out the quick comic aside (mea culpa: that's a line of attack near and dear to my own performing style).

They believe that what they are about to show you is beyond belief; in many cases, it appears to be beyond even what *they* can believe!

You can be sure about this:

Anything you treat as trivial will receive a trivial response.

Did the pen pass through the dollar bill? How did you react? With a smirk? A smile? A look of wonder? A look of relief that it happened?

Your reaction to the moment steers the audience's reaction. Remember, in most cases your onlookers are seeing something for the first time in their lives. Strange as it may seem to us, they need you to help them appreciate your skills.

Let me explain. Can you juggle? If you can, you know that juggling three rubber balls brings smiles—but juggling three chain saws elicits applause. Juggling three chain saws *while they are running* brings gasps followed by applause. The audience understands, without any help from the performer, that the latter stunt carries a great degree of difficulty—and danger—and they reward the mountebank accordingly.

But when watching a magician, the audience has no reliable frame of reference for difficulty. Which is the more impossible, reaching into the air and producing coins, or bending a spoon by lightly touching it? There can be no answer, for each defies logic and physics.

The Miser's Dream effect can be achieved with pure manual dexterity, while magic catalogues offer a multitude of devices to accomplish the same feat (as perceived by the audience) with little or no sleight of hand required. Which production of money from nothing is better, the "pure" or the mechanical method? Obviously, it depends on the performer's style and the entire framework on which the routine is hung. A spectator has no way of giving credit—or deducting approval—for either method.

Put another way, the spectators have no way of knowing that any particular moment of your show is special.

Unless you tell them.

Kreskin has understood and exploited this insight from the earliest days of his career. When he performs the linking of three borrowed finger rings, he tells the audience, in several different ways, that what they are about to witness is unique, and he will probably take the secret to his grave. And who among the lay people watching can question his statements (outrageous as they may be to magicians)? His version of the trick is special because of the very fact that *he tells them it's special.* Many magicians perform this routine; few make it into a theater-filling moment of high drama. Most magicians reduce it to a good trick at best; goofy, oddball Mr. K. elevates it into an extraordinary occurrence that some witnesses recall years afterward.

On the other hand, the more trivial the trick, the more you must increase the entertainment value of the surrounding routine.

I love seeing or reading about performers who wring solid entertainment from the simplest, *Robbins E-Z Magic* catalog type tricks. It's done everyday. Shopping-mall Svengali Deck hawkers draw in the crowds doing feats that we all know can be learned (technically) in minutes, because their machine-gun patter makes it impossible to look away. They make simple tricks *exciting*.

Which parts of your routines are trivial? Which stand out and will be remembered a week later?

Something special happens in every magic trick. Find it. Emphasize it.

Why should I spend a slice of my life watching you?

4. Control Every Moment

Every moment counts. You cannot permit the minds of your audience to wander.

In tennis (and other sports as well), coaches urge their students to "Play the ball; don't let the ball play you."

Translated to show business, you must play the audience, and never let the audience play you. Every moment when you stand on stage, *you* must control the action. Understand and accept that from time to time gremlins will work their slimy machinations upon your carefully rehearsed program. Don't panic. It's a part of show business to have things go wrong. Screw-ups happen to pros and amateurs alike, and how you handle those moments when the microphone cuts out, or the lights flicker, or you realize you pulled the wrong cards out of your pocket, are moments that separate the winners from the losers in show biz.

Nothing ruins a show faster than when your audience knows, or even suspects, that you have lost control of the moment.

Understanding that truism, you must gird yourself to *never lose control.* Disciplined practice sessions and performing experience will always be the best teachers in these situations, but you can ease the learning process by preparing for the worst.

Here are a few tricks of the trade to help you maintain control.

Use a Lower Gear for More Traction

If you do sense that the bond between you and your audience has too much slack, you can do what many performers do: increase your energy level (speed things up). Or better yet, you can slow down.

You may be surprised that I urge you to slow down. In fact, that was one of the best tips I learned back in my college theater days, and I have used it often. When I feel the audience's attention on me is slipping away, it frequently is because I've been running for too long at one level: high energy. By simply s-l-o-w-i-n-g d-o-w-n, and lowering the volume and pitch of my voice, the audience snaps to attention.

The change of pace, and nothing else, alerts them that something new is happening on stage. Frequently, that's all I need to put me back in command.

I recall seeing a performance by Anton Zellman, one of the leading, and highest-paid, trade-show producers and performers in America. He is a super-smooth showman (in the best sense) and his memory and mentalism demonstrations pull in the crowds from the trade-show aisles. On this particular night he was doing a stage show. In every way, it was up to his high standards. But then he called up to the stage a woman who is the wife of an old friend of his and the texture of the show changed... for the better. Suddenly he began talking conversationally, as opposed to the precision-made speech patterns he used up until that point. I could feel within the audience around me a renewed and heightened interest in the performance, and it was due, I believe, to his softer, friendlier, and, yes, slower voice.

It would have been a mistake for him to have used this voice throughout the program. It was the *contrast* that brought the audience's attention to a new, higher level, one that would not have been achieved had he continued to perform all the way through with his usual high-energy approach.

I acknowledge that the more common fault is working or talking too slowly. In the next section, "Eliminate Weak Spots," we'll examine how to know when you've got to speed up, and how to do it correctly.

And then I, ummm, like, said to the guy...

You lose a bit of control every time you insert hesitation into your speech pattern. Every ummm, uhhh, ehhh, drawn-out "well," or any of their many equivalents, immediately tells the audience that you have, however briefly, lost your way.

Avoiding those hesitations is not a difficult skill to acquire. First, acknowledge your tendency to speak the way we all speak in social situations. And then recognize that performing demands a higher degree of fluency. Putting it succinctly, your awareness of the problem is more than half the solution.

When you reach a moment when you are unsure about what to say next... *pause*! You will sound thoughtful and wise. Insert an ummm, and you sound, well, ummm, how should I put this? Let's see... ummm, well, like one of those nice, but regular folks out there in the audience. After all, *they* could get up on stage and sound frightened and unsure and wimpy—and not in control of that moment.

Is that what you want? Hell, no! Make sure *you* don't sound like that. S-l-o-w d-o-w-n and think, if you must, but never let them know, not even for a split second, that you have lost control of your own speech patterns.

A facile and confident flow of words is inextricably related to the time you spend rehearsing your script, and we discuss this in greater detail in the chapter on Scripting.

Superman doesn't hem and haw. Clark Kent does. Which are you?

Never Apologize to Your Audience

Remember, *they don't care.* Entertainment is about escaping reality, so resist the temptation to explain your problems. *They don't care.* You are Superman, and Superman doesn't suffer from colds or backaches, from lack of sleep. They don't care about problems backstage, or that your kids kept you up last night, or about any illness or other personal problems. And you should never send their attention to any glitches in the sound or lighting systems, as many performers do.

The temptation to apologize or explain can be huge and compelling. I know from experience. I've had backaches that made me wince with every step. I performed days after my mother died when I was only twenty-six years old. I have chronic asthma and once in a while it kicks up during a show. I've gone on with no sleep in days, with high fever, with stomach cramps, with severe allergies (not all in the same day!). For those reasons and more, I want them to know why I might have a bit less energy than usual, and I've told them, and only after too many years did it finally sink in: *they don't care!*

Not only do they not care, but by apologizing or explaining away some problem, you lower yourself a notch. An apology is Kryptonite to your Superman image: it weakens you.

There are two exceptions: 1) you apologize because you must, or 2) you apologize to get a laugh.

If the start of your show has been delayed beyond a reasonable time, you offer a simple, direct apology in order to negate negative vibes. That's an apology with a purpose.

If something is *obviously* out-of-the-ordinary—you're wearing a cast on your arm, you're limping, you have laryngitis, you're performing in street clothes because your suitcase was stolen—then you have a reason to offer an apology. So you do it—succinctly, and with humor if possible.

Or you apologize for a punch line.

Kreskin explains to his audience, early in his show, that he bumped into a ladder ("a ladder moved in front of me") and hurt his knee. Then he says, "You're probably thinking to yourself, 'If Kreskin is such a great mentalist, why didn't he see the ladder coming?'" Kreskin has used this gag for years, so there must be a purpose. And the purpose is clear: he gets a laugh while at the same time he acknowledges his fallibility— a useful ploy at the beginning of a 90-minute mentalism set.

Now, as Kreskin might say, "I know what you're thinking." You're thinking that the advice to Never Apologize doesn't mesh with Establish Your Humanity. Not true. You *Establish Your Humanity* in a planned, deliberate manner, a manner that reveals who you are... in the best light, of course. Apologizing for external problems brings you down a notch, down into the audience, and you never want to drop down (figuratively) and join the audience. They should be looking up to you, literally *and* figuratively.

And certainly, never apologize for cutting something from your act. No one knows what you intended to do, so why tease them?

Radiate Control

From the moment you walk in front of the audience, you want them at ease with you. People feel comfortable when they believe they are in the presence of someone who knows what he's doing, who sends out vibes that say, "I'm your Captain, I'm in command, and you can place your confidence in me."

Anything that sends signals of insecurity must be avoided. Here are a few tips for avoiding telltale signs of a person not in control (you can check for them on your videotape):

- Don't pace! Walking back and forth as you talk signals insecurity. Stand your ground. When you do move, move with a purpose. Anchor yourself, internally and externally.
- Don't shift your weight nervously from side to side.
- Don't sway or rock.
- Don't fidget with the microphone, the mike stand, the cards or any prop. In fact, you should avoid touching anything—your table, the lectern, props, volunteers— until the moment you need to. A touch should be a deliberate and necessary motion.
- Don't keep your hands jammed in your pockets.
- Don't repetitively clear your throat or cough nervously.

Are You Looking At Me?

You can maintain control with your gaze. In fact, you *must* be aware of the *entire* room. Continually scan the audience, not only for the eye contact, but also to ensure that the people on the periphery remain as involved as those up closer to you. As soon as you do see anyone drifting away—mentally or physically—pump up your attention to that section of the room. Make them aware—without doing anything that may be obvious to the others in the audience—that you're bringing them back into the action.

Here's how:

• Look at them just a bit longer as you talk.

• Smile directly at them.

• If you reach a moment when you would normally make a gesture out toward the audience, allow your arm to point in their direction for just an extra second or two.

Unless they're sloshed or otherwise oblivious, they'll usually get the message.

Excuse Me?

For stage workers especially—except for when it suits your purpose—never respond to an intentional interruption from the audience: a question, a statement, a joke, or any remark from a heckler. Because if you do respond, you grant permission for the next interruption.

I have seen too many performers break the flow of their act by needlessly, and unproductively, responding to something that didn't require a response. Don't fall into that easy trap. Unless you have developed a rapier wit and sure-fire comebacks, ignore, ignore, *ignore*, despite the temptation to appear witty or friendly.

This advice is less viable for close-up workers, especially table-hoppers; after all, you've encroached on their territory. In that case it's you, not they, who must fit into the flow and ambience of the setting.

Dominate Me. I Like It!

And finally, you Control Every Moment because that's what your audience craves.

People have humdrum little lives—or as Thoreau said, "lives of quiet desperation"—and they have real problems and crave a release (however temporary) from their everyday ennui. They want to connect with the possibility that there actually might be a Superman who can accomplish miracles. That's what Houdini gave his audiences and that's why he became so much more than a music-hall entertainer.

People want to believe there is something beyond, a something that imposes its own order upon the universe. By controlling your environment in a way they cannot, you give your audience optimism and, perhaps, something to which they themselves might aspire.

5. Eliminate Weak Spots

Here's an interesting, highly generalized observation: amateur magicians perform too slowly, and *advanced* amateurs and newbie professionals perform too quickly.

The amateurs perform slowly because they fail to put in the requisite rehearsal time and practice, and so they end up fishing for the right words. Or the right cards. Or birds.

Advanced amateurs and new pros perform too quickly because they have not yet developed confidence in the impact of their routines.

Before we go further, let me be crystal-ball-clear about my position here: *Faster is almost always better than slower.*

Slow works only if you have the audience fully fixated on your every word and action. Slow is much more difficult to pull off successfully, but slow can be much more effective. More on that later.

For the most part, if you successfully erect the first four Pillars, you won't *have* weak spots. For the most part.

Eliminating weak spots may become the biggest payoff of videotaping your performance. Once you have a tape and can see what the audience sees and hears, you can begin intelligently to gauge the flow of your program.

As you watch yourself on tape, be prepared to edit your act ruthlessly. Chop out unnecessary words, delete sentences that fail to move the routine forward, demolish whole routines if they fail to get the hoped-for response.

Make every moment important to the flow of the entertainment. Not *most* moments. *Every* moment. *Every second.*

Watch each segment of your show over and over. With repeated viewings, you begin to see the flaws, the needless words, the hesitations that impede the flow. Use the remote control aggressively to break your performance down into ever-smaller segments: five minutes, three minutes, thirty seconds.

You think that's asking too much? Consider the musician, who follows a precise set of instructions—hundreds or thousands of notes—each thoughtfully placed to build upon the preceding note. Every note, encompassing a tiny slice of time, demands precision. A false note jars the senses and ruins the effect of the music, so the musician rehearses the task of perfecting these minuscule moments in order to achieve the perfect whole.

Why should magicians do less?

When I say that you must consider every second, I'm neither kidding nor engaging in hyperbole.

To illustrate a couple of examples of missed opportunities, I'll describe part of what you can see on *"Spectators Don't Exist,"* a video of above-average table-hopping routines put out by English magician Jon Allen (major kudos to Jon, by the way, for showing us his routines performed out in the real world for unsuspecting people; would that all magic videos did the same).

In a floating dollar bill routine he calls "Ghost," he starts by asking, "Do you believe in ghosts or anything like that?" He gets a couple of mild responses and then never brings up anything about ghosts again. Obviously, he intends to imply that a spirit of some sort makes the bill move, but he fails to communicate that to the viewers. He should either follow up on that theme or not bring it up initially.

He asks that the borrowed bill be signed, and while that happens he takes a wine glass from the table, turns it upside-down away from the table to spill out any last drops and says to no one in particular, "I'll make sure this is empty and dry; I could drink it but I won't...," and then places it back down. It's a few meaningless words, a few weak seconds in which nothing is accomplished.

Perhaps he could be more proactive in that moment, possibly by looking at the woman whose glass he is taking and saying something like, "That's a perfect ghost trap! May I borrow it for a moment?" Almost anything that keeps him in control of that moment will play stronger than turning away and talking to himself.

The missed opportunity to control that moment lasted just three or four seconds, and the balance of the routine played well. Most magicians would be thrilled to get the reaction Mr. Allen achieves. My point here, and throughout this book, is that good is never enough.

Raise your level.

Speed Kills

Years ago I read one jazz critic's assessment of how you can tell good musicians from great musicians. The good ones dazzle listeners by playing notes with blinding speed, while the greatest musicians play only the necessary notes.

It's the same in magic. We have no shortage of technically skilled practitioners, top-gun fly-boys who seek to dazzle us with their rat-tat-tat displays of deft sleights and flourishes. And we have a surfeit of word wizards who ply us with bada-boom bada-bing patter, rarely pausing to let the audience catch up and appreciate their cleverness. Both can entertain audiences, and be labeled good or very good. More commonly, however, we see speed demons smash one moment into the next, and their spectators lose interest. ("A blur of great magic is still a blur.") When that happens, the magician will be at a complete loss to understand why repeat bookings don't materialize.

You will have weak moments if you try too hard to impress. If you tend to move along at a fast clip, that may be, for you, vastly better than allowing the pace to flag. Just be aware that in a longer show, say fifteen minutes or more, you may want to slow down now and then, not only to change the texture of the program, but also to allow yourself to play the necessary notes, those that deliver the strongest emotional punch.

Excepting those born and raised in the Southern part of the United States, the majority of professional magicians speak too quickly (I know that's a tendency I personally must constantly guard against). It's probably because we know the words, we've thought about them over and over. And familiarity breeds speed.

The spectator is hearing your words for the first time. Don't garble them. Don't rush them. Watch your tape and listen to yourself as a spectator listens. Try to judge if every word is intelligible.

The Pause that Refreshes

Pauses, at the right time, and done with a sense of control, add power.

Never confuse an intentional pause with a weak spot. A moment is weak if it adds no meaning to the effect. In a strong routine, there may be moments when no one speaks, but never "dead" silence. Silence is deafening if you are searching for a prop or you are at a loss for words.

On the other hand, a dramatic pause just prior to the climactic moment may be the final booster rocket needed to launch the effect into a higher orbit.

You may not enjoy reading this, but not everyone pays attention to your every word. Minds wander. Attention becomes diffused in spite of, or sometime because of, intensity. People fall asleep at rock concerts because of the sameness of the sound level, just as people fall asleep while the TV blares but then wake up when the loving spouse turns it off.

A pause in your act is the TV being shut off. It jolts. And it can jolt your audience in a manner beneficial to your success.

Pauses also become effective when used to signal the inner struggle—the difficulty—of the moment. And we must never lose sight of the struggle; after all, if failure is not a possibility, what's the point?

The Magic is Rarely Enough

Finally, you will have slow spots if all you have going for you is the magic, because the magic is rarely enough. You're going to amaze me? OK, and what else?

Within seconds after the Amazing Jonathan walks out, it's clear that he's going to make me laugh... and amaze me. David Copperfield and Siegfried & Roy dazzle me... and amaze me. Lance Burton charms me... and amazes me. David Blaine dramatically transfixes me... and amazes me. Kreskin tells me fascinating (for the most part) stories about his long career and about the human mind... and amazes me.

It goes back to: what *Reaction* do you want from each moment? The climax is just one part, often a small part, of any trick. Magic at magic conventions is so often boring precisely because the routine has been crafted to showcase the "magic" with little thought or effort going into the "everything else."

The magic is rarely enough.

You will lose your audiences if you expect them to wait patiently for the payoff.

6. Build to a Climax

"Always leave 'em wanting more" is a show biz saying that needs to be rethought. The original intent is correct—you never want to overextend your welcome. But you cannot leave your audience "wanting more" because you failed to provide a clear-cut conclusion. If your act is a conveyor belt of tricks, and it suddenly *stops*, your spectators will feel cheated; they want more, they want a final punctuation, a "period," (or better yet, an exclamation point) that gratifies, satisfies, and fulfills their expectations of your entertainment experience.

That's why each routine must build, internally, to a climax, and the entire act must build, inexorably, to its highest point.

To an outsider, and certainly to many magicians, it would seem that the very nature of magic makes the advice to build to a climax with each trick superfluous. After all, every trick comes with a built-in climax: your hand is empty, now there's a coin in it. A card is selected, and then it rises from the deck. Setup, climax. One follows the other.

So on the surface, the advice to Build to a Climax may seem unnecessary. It's not. There's a huge difference between *having* a climax and *building* to a climax. Too many performers make the assumption that the audience will, in essence, climax with the performer.

Well, in magic and in lovemaking, there's a chasm between real life and what you read in the magazines.

Each trick must be thoughtfully constructed to build, as with an old-fashioned wooden roller coaster—click-click-click—anticipation. And the program as a whole must send them back to their lives with a blast-in-the-face rush.

Although this section stresses the importance of your final routine, in truth it's typically more difficult to find ideal openers. Your first few moments set the tone, telegraph your style, and cause the audience to decide if they're going to psychically invest themselves in your performance. Ironically, while finding your ideal opening effect may take years, an experienced performer could theoretically mold almost any piece of decent magic into a strong climax. For example, I've read that Michael Skinner developed a dynamite routine with the classic "toy" magic trick, the Ball and Vase. A Svengali Deck could be the basis of a dramatic blindfold card stab routine. Truly, any effect that usually receives a strong reaction can be your climax, if you properly ramp up the presentation.

Surprisingly to some, the climax of your show is not necessarily your most amazing effect. In fact, sometimes there's no effect at all at the end! The climaxes of some of the best shows I've seen are nothing more than the performer gathering all the warmth and energy in the room and placing it upon himself. In one of my Personal Entertainment Highlights, for example, you'll read how consummate mentalist Gil Eagles dramatically closes his show with the removal of a blindfold. No fireworks, no music, no wham-bang "closer." Just a slowing down of the excitement with a commensurate outpouring of affection from performer to audience, and from audience to performer. It's quiet, but it's a rush nonetheless.

Simply put: for any climax to be effective it must be set apart from the body of the show.

I can't design a killer climax for you, but I can provide some basic guidelines:

- If you perform at a leisurely pace, increase the energy.
- If most of your show is fast-paced, slow down.
- If you use music, either stop the music (temporarily) or dramatically change the music.
- If you don't use music, bring music in at the finale.

And other techniques:

- A reprise of an earlier feat, but this time with a twist
  - Faster (or slower)
  - More difficult (new hurdles to overcome)
- A return to "failures" or "mistakes" which had been done straight or as gags, and are now brought to successful conclusions.

Whatever you do, make certain that your last minutes with the audience stand apart from all that came before. Even simply announcing, "I'd like to close my show for you tonight..." may serve the purpose perfectly. It sets up the expectation that something extra-special is about to unfold, so close attention needs to be paid.

Vary the Texture

A number of leading magic writers forcefully contend that, in structuring your act, it's of the utmost importance that each section appear progressively more difficult. Bull! Each section has to flow into the next, and each must stand on its own. If a particular piece increases the suspense, or supposed difficulty, that's fine, but achieving an interesting texture for your performance as a whole is the desired goal. You can still build toward your final climax by using various moods, each having its own charm, or power, or fascination.

Copperfield, as with many other illusionists, typically starts with a startling appearance; later on in the show he moves to quiet close-up routines or silly kid-show stuff (albeit high-end, silly kid-show stuff). He is *not* progressively performing more difficult or impressive feats.

Gourmet chefs find the right mix of textures and colors: sweet against acidic, crunchy atop velvety. We too need to throw surprises onto the plate. Forcing yourself to make each trick stronger and more powerful as the show progresses can be counterproductive. Focus instead on making each piece fit the whole, the flow, the desired internal structure, with the understanding that the audience fully expects your final piece to be your best.

Heighten the Impossibility

When discussing climaxes we must look back to Capture the Excitement. You will build the best climax to any trick by carefully extracting the moment where the magic happens, and whenever possible, helping the audience to understand why what they are about to see is... impossible.

Experienced performers instinctively know, or learn, how to ratchet up the drama. Among the infinite pick-a-card tricks, virtually all start with the performer either knowing the identity of the card prior to its selection, or learning the identity or location of the card within seconds of its return to the deck. At that point, the issue is: how will I reveal what I know? You could simply announce, "You chose the Three of Spades."

Yeah, you could, but you won't.

Or you could take the spectator's wrist and—by giving careful instructions for her to first think of the color, then the suit, then the value—attempt to ascertain the identity of the card by your highly developed ability to read clues from her pulse. Same trick, but now you have built a little playlet and heightened the perceived difficulty.

Almost any trick can be made stronger simply by thinking about how you can make it appear more difficult, more impossible.

Ricky Jay closed his Off-Broadway hit show, *On The Stem*, with a multiple card-selection routine. It's nothing more than a string of standard pick-a-card/here's-your-card effects. But there's nothing run-of-the-mill in the way Ricky builds the pace, the drama and bang-bang-*bang!* excitement with each revelation.

Lance Burton is a master at Communicating his Humanity, a talent he called upon for the climax of his first TV special. He just sat on a stool, center stage, talking softly to the audience as he performed a charming torn-and-restored newspaper. No flash, no explosions, no monster trick, just one human sharing a moment with his audience. And it worked beautifully.

John Carney, in his outstanding contribution to the literature, *The Book of Secrets*, tells of a significant lesson he learned from the late Michael Skinner. It had to do with what Skinner called "The Magic Moment," that instant in a routine when the magic happens as a result of something the magician does.

> *Sometimes Michael would create an anticipatory tension in what he would call the "exaggerated pause." Just previous to revealing the vanish of a coin or the change of a card, he would sometimes stop still and quiet, his hands hovering frozen over the object. He would hold this pause for five seconds or more, to the point where the silence felt almost uncomfortable. He would then snap his fingers and reveal the effect of his intense concentration. The dramatic suspense created by this pause provided a focus and anticipation that increased the effect many times over. In this way, he had made it known that this phenomenon had not just randomly occurred. As a magician, he had caused it to happen. He had created a "magic moment."*

Carney called Skinner "the finest all-around sleight-of-hand magician in the world," and it's clear that Skinner understood the overarching concepts required to successfully entertain with close-up magic. Those concepts apply equally well to all other branches of magic.

Skinner, in concert with all the best magicians, didn't throw away the moment of magic; he built up to it and presented it on a silver platter. *Here* is the *magic!*

On Multiple Climaxes

In multi-phase routines, or multi-climax routines, there must be a dramatic progression. Magicians love *Matrix* assembly-type effects. I wonder if we're fooling ourselves about the true impact of any effect loaded with mini-climaxes. What's the point? That a coin travels invisibly from under this card to that card, again and again? Or are we demonstrating our dexterity? In either case, the entertainment value—the surprise moment—is diminished with each revelation. You cannot simply keep doing the same thing over and over and expect the audience to care.

Here's what John Northern Hilliard had to say on this topic in his classic book, *Greater Magic*:

> *[The] Tarbell rope trick, although a masterpiece of magic, has a weak finish because you have repeated cutting and restoring two or three times. Where is your climax? The first restoration is the surprise moment, the second and third are repeats of the same surprise and are, therefore, less surprising each time. All these new tricks of twisting and turning yards of rope, with dozens of loops, don't mean a thing from an audience point of view. The simpler the trick, the better. You have a rope, you cut it in two, rejoin it and throw it out. Finished! No loops, no complicated moves, apparently just a little miracle.*

I have seen a few presentations of the *Matrix* type of effect and (fewer still) long rope tricks that were entertaining, so it is possible to pull it off. For any multi-climax trick to be effective, though, there must be something beyond repetitive magic, and usually that something is *fun*. When fun equals or exceeds the magic, you hold the viewer's attention.

One of the best examples of this is a beautifully presented version of the *Miser's Dream*. In my first "Personal Entertainment Highlights," there's a snippet about Al Flosso's presentation of this classic. He did the same trick many times, producing coins from impossible places, but the element of great fun—and surprise—never left the routine.

In the Denny & Lee Performance video (from dennymagic.com), you can see how Denny and Lee take a piece of standard "box magic," the Substitution Trunk, and without excess glitter or speed turn it into an ovation-inducing finale.

Slow? In the time it took for the metamorphosis to take place, the Pendragons could do their act, cook dinner and vacuum the den. Yet the audience gave Denny and Lee an enthusiastic standing ovation. Why? Denny's handling of this classic completely lacks the speed and finesse so common among TV-special magicians. Instead of speed, he emphasizes the *impossibility* of the stunt. At his insistence, male volunteers banged and slapped away at all sides of the wooden crate. They checked out the canvas bag, and the rope, and the locks. And at the end, when Denny emerges from the canvas bag, a palpable sense of *Wow!* courses through the audience.

In sum, it comes down to this: the Pendragons communicate a show that says, "Look how cool *we* are!" There's nothing wrong with cool. The public wants to see cool people. That's why *People* magazine exists.

Denny and Lee, on the other hand, implicitly ask, "Do you want to see something really *amazing*?"

The Pendragons take your breath away; it takes longer to say "instantaneous" than for the switch to occur. They deserve all their accolades. I just want you to be aware that the trappings of a full Las Vegas main-stage act are not required to thoroughly entertain your audience, and that you can take a piece of "standard" magic and build it into an ovation-producing climax.

One True Climax Per Audience, Thank You

While some performers lack a strong climax for their show, others make the equally egregious mistake of having more than one; that is, they set the audience up to believe they are seeing the grand moment, and then the program moves on to yet another, unrelated trick. That's a big mistake.

You can take the audience to the mountaintop only once. Keep going, and you risk falling off the edge. When I watch a movie, a play, or a magic act, I feel slightly cheated when I realize the climax ain't the climax; I have invested emotional collateral in that moment, and then, when it's clear there's more to come, I hold back from fully enjoying the next "climax" because I've been burned once.

All's Well That Ends Well

Shakespeare, as usual, figured it all out. If your show ends on an up beat—if your audience is thrilled, laughing, crying from heartfelt emotion, astonished to a degree that takes them beyond all that has gone before—*you win*. Mistakes are forgotten, *faux pas* recede from memory, launched into obscurity by the thrust of your climactic moments. We humans are a forgiving lot. Make us feel good before you send us back to our real lives, and you will be remembered fondly.

That is why you invest extra time, effort and creativity into delivering the absolutely strongest climax possible.

Nail your climax!

* * *

There you have it: the Six Pillars of Entertainment Success—specifically for *magicians* and *mentalists*. Yes, an enlivened government-policy wonk grandmother can enthrall her investment-professional audience without *Capturing the Excitement* or *Building to a Climax*.

We cannot.

For us, to achieve *maximum* entertainment, we need all six.

A Personal Entertainment Highlight:
Sylvester the Jester

To label a performer unique is generally to be clichéd and hyperbolic, not to mention wrong. Until you encounter Sylvester the Jester.

I had seen his cartoon-comes-to-life act on television and I remember being impressed. Then I saw him live at a magic convention and I was blown away by his manic and thoroughly magical inventiveness. Then I saw him do superbly mystifying and hilarious close-up *in character* and I was impressed even more!

And then he sat with me at lunch and did his Sylvester Pitch: the continuous production of, well, just about anything that can fit in a hand, an arm's length from my face, and I realized this guy comes from a different gene pool than the rest of us.

The uniqueness of his stage character, the perfect meshing of his one-of-a-kind magic, done flawlessly with music, sets, and costumes, leaves me breathless. And when he lectures to magicians about his amazing vest (a device he designed and built on his own), from whence pour all the hilarious cartoon sounds, it underlines how trite the word "creative" truly can be when applied to most of us.

Perhaps you're wondering how he can Communicate His Humanity while "hiding" behind the cartoon character. Well, 'toons have feelings too! We empathize with him as he gets pulled and squished and maimed in unfathomable ways. And we laugh with him when he overcomes all manner of misfortune.

He is truly, amazingly *unique*.

Section III

# ◀ PREPARATION ▶

*"The state of having been made
ready beforehand; readiness."*

Chapter 5
Scripting and Rehearsing

Writing a Script: Just Do It

Industrial shows occupy a unique niche in show business. Some of the most talented actors, writers, singers, dancers, and musicians in the land specialize in this branch of the business, and can earn excellent money without making a dent in the public consciousness. From time to time, a firm hires an actor to play a magician for one of these gigs. He learns the script (frequently written by a magician), does the show, and moves on in his career. For him, the role of being a magician is merely another job.

For every other person who sees themselves as a magician, the pursuit of magic began, with varying degrees of passion, as a hobby, a pleasurable pastime. Something you would do for free (shhh, don't let outsiders know that).

Now here comes Weber saying you should write out a script for your performance. Not only that, I'm exhorting you to expend as much effort on your script as the writers of the industrial shows do for their non-magician actors.

Yes, I know; that smells like work. And *work* don't jibe with *hobby*.

"I won't do it, I tell ya!"

Calm down, and let me tell you why you must.

In my own life, in both my business and entertainment careers, I always rebelled against the common advice to:

"List your goals, your strengths, your weaknesses."

"Write down where you see yourself in five years."

"Name the five biggest roadblocks to your success.

Yada, yada, yada. For years, anything that remotely smacked of New Age psychobabble, even these modest requests to focus my energies, sent me into a fit of I-don't-need-to-do-this-crap.

My mistake. Looking back, I now sheepishly admit to myself that the times I *did* get off the couch and write things down *always* paid off. Big time.

Writing a script forces you to think, slowly, word by torturously-pulled-from-your-brain word, about where you're headed, and what your audience should expect from you. The physical act of putting words on paper prevents you from going from Point A to Point C without considering Point B.

So get your routines down on paper. It may not be fun, but do it. Do it carefully, writing down both the words you will say—the dialogue—and the actions you will take. Later, after a few hours at least—or better yet, after a few days—go back to your written words and you will see them with a fresher perspective.

In my financial business, I write a good deal of marketing material. Every time I write a new marketing piece, I'm certain that it's a gem at birth—and then I look at it a few days later and wonder, "What the hell was I thinking?" Time works in your favor as your thoughts marinate in your skull. Your subconscious mind dices and chops, and invents variations on the original theme.

If you don't write a script, details will most certainly escape, and those details can make the difference between good and *great*.

Be a Marksman with Your Words

Remember the Big Three reactions? Every sentence you utter, every word, should be aimed at one of these narrowly defined targets:

1. **Rapt Attention**
2. **Astonishment**
3. **Laughter**

Plus, when absolutely required:

4. **Necessary Instructions or Explanations**

That's it. Anything *not* fitting one of these targets is most likely fluff that hurts your show. And I mean *anything*: unnecessary words weigh you down and dilute your impact.

As you write and rewrite your script, check it against the four targets. Edit out as much as you can without causing severe damage to the routine.

Remember also that *clarity of purpose* is essential to achieving the third *Pillar of Entertainment Success* ("Capture the Excitement"). Choose and structure routines so that no doubts linger about what you are doing and why you are doing it. You dampen excitement if the audience is confused about *anything*.

Actions and Dialogue

When you write your script, you must include the words you say and the actions you will take. If you really get serious about this, you might invest in specialized scriptwriting software to facilitate the process, but for most performers any good word-processing program will suffice.

Don't neglect the actions. Sure, Shakespeare left us almost no stage directions, but you ain't no Bard of Avon. The more detailed your script, the better. Again, the aim here is to get you thinking about the minutiae that at first may seem unimportant.

Is the egg bag in your left hand or your right? If it's in your right hand, and you invite a spectator up on stage, you must transfer it to your left at some point so you can shake hands. Do you want to do that? Will it look as though you are doing something sneaky during the transfer? Perhaps it's better to have the bag in your left hand earlier. Where do you want the spectator to stand? That may depend on whether she'll be asked to reach into the bag. And since most people are right-handed, do you want her to extend her arm out to the side, or will she be forced to cross over her body, which may cause her to turn sideways to the audience. Is that OK, or not?

Details, details. The more you consider at this point, the fewer surprises are likely to pop up and bite your butt in front of strangers.

Once you've finished the writing, read your dialogue *out loud*.

Then read it aloud again.

And again.

It's part of rehearsing, so you need to do this anyway. Each time you go through this exercise, vary some aspect of the reading. Change the pace, search for awkward phrasings and opportunities for humor, think about what might be extraneous to the action, and what might enhance it.

When it starts to feel comfortable, get out your tape recorder.

Speak exactly as you will on stage: same pacing, same inflections, same pauses, same projection. If you've never done this before, you will likely feel terribly self-conscious and awkward. That's normal. Plow ahead anyway. Each time you record yourself, the task becomes easier.

Now leave it alone for a few days. When you go back and listen to yourself, close your eyes and become your audience.

Let the Analysis Begin

Do you sound natural? If you detect even a hint of artifice or forced humor, note it on paper immediately, but continue listening so you get a full overview of the presentation. Then start reworking—*by rewriting*—the dialogue.

And for best results, repeat the process.

Reverse Engineering

We all have routines that we've been performing for some time. In such cases, it's useful to tape the performance and then transcribe your words onto paper (or, more realistically, a computer screen). This exercise is especially useful for close-up and walk-around performers who may not easily be able to videotape their acts.

You can't assume that, merely because you've done a routine many times, it's reached its highest level of perfection. Seeing the words on paper will offer a new perspective, and an opportunity to infuse new life into the performance.

Once you've transcribed the routine, the process becomes the same as for a new routine: analyze, rewrite, re-record.

Actions

In addition to the words you will speak, write out—in as much detail as you can muster—all the actions you will perform on stage.

Assume you're going to force a name using a change bag. If you're lazy and look for shortcuts, you might write your script this way:

I hold up the transparent change bag; spectator reaches into bag and removes one slip.

Well, that's better than writing nothing down at all. *Now let's assume you take performing seriously.* In that case, your script for the same sequence might read:

Spectator stands on my right. I hold up change bag in both hands and glance to see that the force side is facing spectator.

"In a moment, I'm going to turn away. When I do, I want you to reach into the bag with your left hand, remove one slip of paper, and then, without looking at it, place it into any one of your pockets. Are you ready to reach into the bag? OK. I'll turn away."

I turn my head to the left.

"Now you turn away." (She will probably miss the bag because she's now not looking.)

"No, no, get your hand in the bag first, otherwise you'll keep missing!"

When I feel her hand in the bag, with my head still turned away:

"Do you have one slip of paper? Are you sure it's only one? OK, now place it into one of your pockets. Have you done that?"

Details, details. Sweat the details. There's no downside to careful planning at this stage.

For My Next Trick, I Have a Deck of Cards Somewhere...

You must pay particular attention to your transitions. The change-over from trick to trick is your Achilles' heel. You become most vulnerable to losing the attention of your audience when you release the dramatic tension (the climax) and then proceed into new territory. Preparation for—and scripting of—these moments is your only shield.

Therefore, when writing out your words and actions, consider:

- What are you going to say in each transition between tricks? You *cannot* simply put props away and then have dead time while you pick up the props for the next bit of business. You must do or say something to keep the audience focused on you. You must control these moments.
- Where are the props for the trick just ended? Write out how to dispose of them.
- Where are the props for the next trick? Specify how you get to them.

The goal is to have your transitions as interesting, as entertaining as the tricks themselves. Not easy, but the best pros do it.

Do you?

Thanks for the Memorize

Some performers worry that committing a script to memory removes the spontaneity. That should be a groundless fear. First, virtually all successful performers, actors, magicians, and comedians say the same words, in more or less the same way, night after night. They have mastered the art of making the rehearsed sound fresh. (You will learn some of their tricks of the trade in the chapter on *Your Voice.*) Second, locking the words into your brain is the very thing that allows you to veer intentionally off course now and then, secure in the knowledge that you can scamper back to your meticulously thought-out script.

When rehearsing your script, you must practice saying your lines aloud. At first, you *will* feel self-conscious. Get over it. There is no way around it. Merely hearing the lines in your head never suffices, because speaking requires some degree of breath control, and that, however minutely, affects your body.

Your movements must become inextricably linked to your patter. And vice versa. Practice to the point that patter automatically triggers moves, and moves trigger specific words.

As I point out in the section on "Control Every Moment" (part of the *Six Pillars* chapter), you must consciously avoid words and sounds that reveal uncertainty: "ummm, uhhh, well," and so on. The ability to have your words flow smoothly from your mouth comes directly from the time you spend rehearsing.

For many, "rehearsing" means going over the words in your mind. That's not good enough! You have to say the words aloud, preferably into a tape recorder. And once you feel your script is complete, you should get into the habit of rehearsing *without stopping*. No matter what, keep going. You need to learn to think on your feet, (or, for you table workers, on your butt) and part of that training is pushing through the stumbles. Each time you do it, you'll improve your ability to improvise.

Practice is the repetition of the actions, the moves. *Rehearsal* is the repetition of everything the audience sees and hears. As performers skilled in the art of deception, we practice the tiniest of movements, repeatedly, until that exquisite time when they require no thought at all. Only then can we do what all other performers do: rehearse the entire presentation, and once again, our only goal is a performance that requires an absolute minimum of conscious effort.

Having your presentation as fully memorized and rehearsed as possible is important because, as any experienced performer can attest, we think better when we are relaxed—or at least less terrified.

Ah, the Profound Irony of Magic.

Magic is an art form different from all others in a most fundamental way.

The dancer, the musician, the actor, the graphic artist, the writer all practice and refine their crafts, then send them out into the world with the full intent that you see, feel, hear every nuanced detail of their efforts.

Contrast that with say, a master of the classic pass. Years of solitary development and practice, and it reaches its supreme level of perfection only when no one recognizes its existence!

Damn, that's got to be frustrating!

This dichotomy between private long-term practice and lack of public acknowledgment hurts magic. Here's why: unlike other performing artists, the hours and years mystery artists spend repeating hidden moves—while resulting in strong technique— deprive them of the time necessary to develop presentation skills.

Let's start changing that.

Build a Brick House

The script is your home base, your safe house.

Once you are standing on stage and the give and take with the audience begins, the script can recede. At first, you take baby steps, into the exciting and dangerous world of the extemporaneous remark: the ad-lib.

But wait!

Did your brilliant rejoinder fall flat? No problem. You just mentally dash back to the performer's best friend, your script; born, bred, and nurtured by you—like a Saint Bernard on an Alpine mountain—it stands by patiently, ready to pull you back to safety and coherence.

Chapter 6
Choosing Material and Developing the Act

Magic that pleases magicians is magic that pleases a narrow stratum of society: adolescent boys. For that's what we are. All of us. Your actual age or gender is irrelevant—if you are reading this book you're an adolescent boy. We like figuring stuff out. Puzzles, oddities, and anomalies appeal to us and challenge us in agreeable ways.

But lo, they're not like us, those citizens sitting out there looking up at us expectantly. We have to consciously force ourselves to put aside our own predilections and prejudices and seek out those tricks that have the widest appeal.

Mind Blowing or Mind Numbing

We all recognize that some tricks baffle more than others. Unless you rely totally on comedy, you want to choose the strongest, most powerful effects you can get your hands on.

That may mean making the painful decision to jettison some of your favorite routines.

Which leads to one of the weirdest observations about our magical world. It's the phenomenon that occurs only at magic lectures. The guest speaker performs a trick and polite applause ensues. Then he explains the method—a *really cool* method— and suddenly everyone snaps to attention and begins forming mental images of squeezing this great new effect into his act.

Stop! If the trick itself didn't grab you, that's it! A weak trick remains a weak trick, no matter how brilliant or devious the method. So unless you radically rework the effect into something superior, forget about it. Look elsewhere.

Never perform a trick if your primary motivation—consciously or subconsciously—is the coolness of the method. That's the tail wagging the dog.

Always think about the effect on the audience first, and then consider whether the method leads to entertainment.

Here's Derren Brown's take on this, as seen on his outstanding video for magicians, *The Devil's Picturebook*. The host on the tape refers to the "Oil and Water" card trick as "a classic in magic." Derren responds matter-of-factly, saying, "Magicians seem to like it." Then he adds, "Oil and Water leaves me cold as a plot; it's an example of the cards doing something as opposed to the performer being something or communicating something."

Derren (and Eugene Berger and others as well) has encapsulated an endemic problem in magic: the performance of tricks that put the focus on the props, rather than on the performer. I don't think he meant to be harsh, but in the broadest sense, "Magicians seem to like it," with the "it" being either the props or the cool method, is an indictment of our fraternity I *am* willing to make.

I enjoy Tenyo's puzzle-tricks, but I also recognize that everyone viewing, for example, the Blue Crystal, gives full credit for the mystery to the plastic thing, not the warm-blooded me. (Yes, I know there are now full-blown routines for these props, which purport to return some of the glow to the magician, but I have yet to be convinced of their effectiveness.)

Whether performing a Tenyo trick for one person or a stage-filling illusion for thousands, given a choice between presenting a magical *thing* or a magical *you*, it should be clear which is better. You want all memories of your performance wrapped around *you* and your brilliant talent. They may later recall your dexterity, or your other skills, or your humor, but your overriding goal is to, as Derren says, *be* something or *communicate* something. Something wonderful.

The props and the methods are your slaves. Master them.

Performance Trumps Trick

The trick or routine is just a fragment of the entertainment process. A small fragment.

You probably don't want to hear that; you've spent a fortune on books, props, videos, and conventions, and perhaps even private lessons. You just know that one "killer" effect is all you need to turn you into a star.

But it never works out that way. The trick is important, but performance trumps the trick every time.

Want proof? Take a look at The Amazing Kreskin during his heyday on American TV, a period spanning the 1970s and '80s. He routinely used one of the simplest and, to my mind, least deceptive card forces known. Commonly called "Crossing the Cut," it forces the top card using nothing more than time misdirection. Yet there he was, making miracles out of it... or at least that's what you would have thought from the reactions of the TV talk show hosts.

Or how about Blaine "biting" a quarter? The *trick* part of that effect is just a step up from a department-store magic kit or the Johnson's Products catalog, yet Blaine sells it as if it's a miracle.

On the other hand, any night a magic club meets you can see the latest, greatest, and cleverest techniques, performed to new heights of boredom and ineptitude.

Wonderful tricks stink if performed poorly. Simple tricks astound in the hands of a smart showman.

Performance trumps trick every time. A weak trick can be elevated by a strong performance, never the other way around; weak performances are little improved by the strength of the tricks.

New Tricks, Old Tricks.
My Tricks, Your Tricks.

The familiar American greeting, "Hi, what's new?" invariably elicits the response, "Not much; what's new with you?" Except in a magic shop. Ask "What's new?" there, and the dealer takes you seriously. He springs into action because we in the magic fraternity appear to be allergic to anything "old": old tricks, old jokes, old routines.

How shortsighted of us. New certainly has its place, and our craft requires innovation to thrive. But never overlook a trick or routine merely because it's familiar to *you*.

Your audience does not know what you know.

"Old," in show business, is better interpreted as "tried and tested." Embrace the classics and build on them. Hoary gags and routines live to ripe old ages precisely because they work, and as entertainers, our mission is to show-and-tell things that connect with our audiences. That's more important than "new."

Naturally, not every old chestnut works for every performer in every situation. Use tried and tested routines and gags sparingly, and only those that comfortably fit your style.

As for the argument about "originality," that's a quagmire of scholarship (sloppy or intense), pride, ethics, and commercial interests. Your "improvement" is my theft, or vice versa. Here's what we know for sure: little in any art form is truly original. Everyone builds upon the past. Understand, however, that if you pilfer a line or bit of business without permission, *it is theft*. And in many cases, that theft is unnecessary, because most performers are flattered when asked for permission to use a brief bit of their show. What you don't want to do, ever, is appropriate large chunks of another's act, not only for the reprehensible ethics such actions represent, but also because there's a strong likelihood that the stolen material, which looked so good in the original show, will flop when shoehorned into yours.

In one of my PEA workshops, I said something that was subsequently quoted several times by others: I believe the average American will see a live performance of 0.5 mentalists in his or her lifetime. I also believe the number is only slightly higher for professional close-up and platform magicians, meaning that most Americans will *die* without ever having seen one of us! So a bit of clearheaded pragmatism ought to seep into the discussions around what's completely original and what's not, and which line or bit is mine and which is yours. (I have had major chunks of my act "borrowed" without permission, and, yes, it hurts like hell when someone says to me, "That was just like Mr. Blankety-Blank did here last year." But over the course of a career, I admit, it didn't have a negative impact on me.) Your *job*, if you are being paid, is not to be original; it is to be the best entertainer you can be. Don't sacrifice your entertainment goals for the sake of originality.

Destination: Astonishment

Now, unlike in the past, magicians can see before they buy: even those living in remote regions can order video catalogues or can access online video clips of many tricks being performed, and seeing is almost always superior to reading an ad. Of course, in most cases the dealer demo shows us the mere *potential* of the trick. But not always. I've found several cases where the dealer, through no brilliant insight, manages to demonstrate a routine that rises above more practiced and elaborate presentations. The reason? The trick has been stripped to its bare essentials, and ends up stronger.

I saw a friend of mine, a highly advanced amateur, perform Dean Dill's stunning rope-and-ring penetration, Dean's Box. He preceded it with a brief discussion of the history of spirit cabinets and related topics. It was a good, solid presentation, yet it failed to ignite the sparks he expected. This trick, after all, is an astonishing mystery that, unless they know the specific principle involved, badly fools most magicians. Sometime later I saw a video demo of this trick and I can tell you, the dealer made it much more powerful by simply pointing out the impossibility of what he was about to do, and then doing it.

The dealer headed straight for the "astonishment" reaction, and got it, while the intelligent amateur sidetracked us with less-than-riveting information.

The next time a dealer asks if you would like to see "what's new and exciting," your smartest response might be, "Actually, I'd rather see what's old and proven."

A brief digression: The raging controversy over the value of learning magic from books versus videos is an absurd waste of ink and trees. It's like asking, "Which is better, a knife or a fork?" Both are useful tools in delivering balanced nutrition, and your intake of magic information ought to be similarly balanced between books and videos. Videos show you the result, books provide the rationale. End of digression.

Strong, Stronger, Strongest

The average magician knows hundreds, maybe thousands of tricks. Your audience, sorry to say, may not have time to see them all.

If you're booked to perform for a specified amount of minutes, you've really got to cut back. So with limited time, it makes no sense to display anything less than your "A" material. Fortunately, there's an efficient way to decide which material stays and which gets booted: *watch your audience.*

If you don't feel you can perform and observe at the same time, ask a trusted friend to do it for you. Specifically, ask a friend to pay more attention to the audience than to you, to take mental or actual notes about which tricks garner strong reactions, and which result in wandering eyes and whispered asides.

Once you have a strong act, break in new material gingerly. *And rarely.*

Keep only the killer routines and the funniest bits of business.

And please refrain from using "sucker" tricks. They've become tiresome even to the casual magic fan and they are rarely worth the feeling of resentment, however slight, that they engender. The same can be said for any trick where the magician succeeds and the spectator doesn't; we like them more than the public does.

Props. Get Real!

The days of props that have no counterpart in real life—props that exist solely for a magic act—are numbered. With all the great tricks available to you, it's just dumb to use any contrivance or prop that screams, "The trick happens *here!*"

Blaine uses no overtly magic props; Kreskin has, but rarely. And even in Copperfield's mega-stage show, you see large amounts of recognizable objects: motorcycles, giant "industrial" fans, couches, exploding buildings, and lots of innocent-looking scaffolding.

Recognizable objects, whether for close-up or stage, will always connect more effectively with an audience's psyche than a three-sided screen "adorned with colorful Chinese characters."

Blow up your Botania, deep-six your Dove Pan, and trash your Tear-Away Box!

Exposure: Indecent?

Some magicians, especially over the past few years, steer away from choosing material that has been "exposed" on television. From my perspective, yes, indiscriminate exposure is a bad thing, and the masked morons on television are very bad.

Mentalists, by the implied nature of their extraordinary demonstrations, stand to suffer the most from television exposures. But how many working performers, including mentalists, have ever been truly, irreparably damaged by exposure? Not Uri Geller (who's been "exposed" thousands of times), not David Blaine, not Kreskin, not Marc Salem, and certainly not Dunninger, even when his alleged methods were published on cereal boxes.

Consider this: today, and every day, perhaps a hundred performers will "expose" Slydini's Paper Balls Over the Head. The entire audience, with one notable exception, will see a very clever method for making a wad of paper vanish, and this rampant exposure has been going on for decades!

Yet, ten years from today, you can be certain that it will still be a sure-fire crowd-pleaser.

So let's plug leaks when and where we can, but never lose sight of the fact that it's the performer that makes the trick, not the other way around. Choose your routines because they're dynamite in your hands, and no one will give thought to the clowns behind the masks.

Second that Emotion

Do you know why you vote for one political candidate over another? Or why you choose a particular automobile? You want to tell me you make your choices logically, but study after study shows us that people make decisions emotionally, then justify those decisions logically. The advertising industry is built on that thesis.

Emotions lubricate the gears of the entertainment experience. *Without emotions, you're doing a lecture.* Whenever possible, choose and develop routines that conjure emotions.

Boris Wild, the talented French magician, does an elementary pick-a-card, here's-your-card trick that grows into an emotional bit of theater. I won't give too much away, except to say that he employs lush music and a loving gaze into the eyes of his female participant. The emotion of the moment, with its hint of amorous involvement, lifts this presentation above the prosaic and dry demonstrations we normally see with cards.

What can you do to inject emotion into your material? Finding the hooks is not an easy task; you won't find them in the directions for the tricks you buy. But think about what sights and sounds affect you; chances are good that they might affect others as well.

With thought and imagination, you can overlay an emotional component upon many standard tricks. Is the key that moves in your hand from the house where your aunt died mysteriously? Is that confetti, or a reminiscence of the first time you saw snow?

You goose emotional reaction by using:

• Music
• Stories
  – A time when you were frightened
  – Memories of a lost romance
  – Happy or sad thoughts about pets
• Sights or sounds of a personal nature (from your past or from the generic past of people in the audience)

Audience Participation

Back when I made most of my income from performing on the college circuit, I continually attended conferences of NACA, the National Association of Campus Activities. Sometimes I was chosen to appear as one of the "showcase" acts, and sometimes not, but either way I made it a point to see many of the other performers. The variety of immensely talented people appearing on those shows repeatedly delighted and surprised me. (The public has no clue about the vast number of unknown but hugely talented people out there in the show business universe.) After years of seeing this parade of future stars I noticed that few tactics pleased audiences more than getting them *involved*. Audience participation. Done in almost any manner, it boosts a show to a higher level. Comedians, jugglers, certainly many music acts, and even mimes, creatively concocted methods to turn spectators into participants.

You should too. Not hokey bits that make adults feel as though they're at a kid's show, but quality pieces of business that get them feeling "we're all in this together." I'm not referring here to situations that require one or more volunteers to join you on stage, which, of course, are fine. Rather, I want you to consider bits of business that involve people who remain seated, and which, at best, engage the entire audience.

You'll be in good company. Did you catch the Rolling Stones 2002 concert tour? I saw it as an HBO TV special, and there was Mick, a man who knows a thing or two about crowd control, flapping his head and scrawny arms and leading the Madison Square Garden thousands in a sing-along! You can't always get them to do what you want, but if you try, sometimes they will.

Working as a hypnotist and mentalist, I made frequent use of audience participation. They attempted to send or receive thoughts en masse, or were "trained" to applaud the hypnotized subjects on my cue. These tactics are powerful tools for pulling every audience member into the world you create on stage.

That's why I suggest you look for those tricks and routines that provide the opportunity to bring your show out to the people looking at you. And even when you do use just a few people from the audience, be sure to involve spectators from all parts of the room.

Don't go overboard. Reserve audience participation for special moments within your program.

Warning, Dangerous Tricks: Proceed with Caution

I may well be in the minority, but I *hate* tricks that put someone at risk. I find the idea of putting a volunteer's head in a guillotine offensive, no matter how uproarious the gags. We live in an imperfect world where surgeons, surrounded by other healthcare professionals, remove the healthy kidney, a world where the most brilliant engineers in the world can't design a fail-safe space shuttle. Accidents happen. You just proved to me that the blade slices asunder the head of cabbage. Now I'm supposed to be amused that the poor fellow's neck is in danger? Or is it no danger? What exactly am I supposed to think? Here's what I think, and what is going through the minds of at least some others in the audience: "yeah, it's funny, but what if...?"

Accidents happen.

And I feel only slightly less at ease about Russian Roulette-type routines where it's the performer who's risking death or serious injury while we watch. During the months I've been writing this book I've learned of *two* performers severely injuring their hands while attempting the "covered knife/spike" effect! Yes, it can be argued that much of circus tradition is rooted in "death-defying" acts. Are you in the circus? Is that the image you want? Can you not find equally compelling material that places no human in a dangerous situation? You can if you try.

Three Case Studies

Case Study #1

Ripped & Restored

I could not attend the 2002 SAM Convention in New York, so I asked a friend to pick up something new and amazing for

110

me (I'm not completely immune to the "new and amazing" bug). He returned with a DVD, Yves Doumergue's *Ripped & Restored* from Meir Yedid Magic.

The effect: a card is freely selected, signed, torn into quarters, and then restored, one piece at time. At the end, the card is handed out.

Obviously, I won't tip anything here. I will tell you that it requires very little setup, the moves are not difficult, and it fools everyone. In short, it's a brilliant piece of magic, and if this plot appeals to you at all, you'd be foolish not to buy this DVD.

Now here's the reason I'm writing about this particular routine: the "live performance" shown on the DVD was shot at a close-up session at a magic convention, Magic on Manhattan 2001. As I watched the "performance" section of the video, I suddenly realized I had been there, in that very audience, watching as the video was shot! Yet the routine, done live for me just a few feet from my face, had left me cold, unmoved, and uncaring.

At the time, this book was not yet conceived, so I was truly just another spectator. Certainly, I had no idea how the card healed itself, *but I didn't care.* In the way it was presented, it was a puzzle, and solving the puzzle offered me no reward. Why should I tax my brain?

The performance in many ways was typical of how tricks such as this are presented, and so it becomes useful to break it down into its component moments for closer analysis:

1) Yves had a man in the second row, just off the center aisle, select a card.

2) The man remained seated, and, since I was seated several rows back, I immediately lost contact with the action. The still-seated man was asked to sign the card, and, during the approximately twelve-second signing process, Yves just stood center stage, quietly waiting. (During which time I was probably thinking, "Where am I going for dinner?")

3) The card was returned to Yves, and he tore it into quarters. Hands moved, covering the card for a split second now and then, pieces restored, more hand movements, and the card became fully restored. All accompanied by a line of patter that basically told us what we were seeing.

It lacked drama; it lacked theatrical focus; it lacked any emotional involvement. The patter added nothing interesting to the effect.

Yet once I watched the DVD explanation, I realized that the method, the handling, the subtleties, and the routing of this effect border on brilliant. So without doubt, this has the potential to be a strong piece of magic. (David Copperfield tore and restored a rare baseball trading card on one of his television specials; it was packed with emotional involvement.)

Every piece of magic we perform is a playlet, a little piece of theater. Accordingly, we have to consider exactly what we are trying to communicate with our words or actions: Drama? Farce? Comedy? Tragedy? Spectacle? A playlet must have a climax, and for us that's easy: it's the moment of the magic. But it also needs more: an interesting exposition leading to the climax. The script for Yves' playlet said to me: something interesting *will* happen, but you'll just have to sit quietly, pay close attention to what I'm doing, and you'll be rewarded with a surprise at the end.

That's not enough!

Case Study #2

A version by Daryl (the renowned close-up magician, not my son) of a Larry Jennings "Jacks Sandwich" effect.

This is another clip I first viewed on the L&L website, and a perfect example of magic for magicians. It's executed beautifully, and as cleanly as this method allows. Yet for me, a few points would be deducted from the "artistic merit" score.

The effect: the two one-eyed Jacks are removed from the deck. A card is selected and returned to the pack, which is then shuffled. Daryl holds the two jacks in one hand while the other hand holds the pack. As the cards from the pack are allowed to dribble from his hand to the table, Daryl stabs the Jacks into the falling cards, separates them, and shows the face-down selected card sandwiched between the face-up Jacks.

Let's go over it, moment by moment.

He ribbon spreads the cards on the table.

"Would you do me a small favor? Take any card from the pack..."

"Would you do me a small favor?" in the middle of a formal routine is an overly and falsely friendly phrasing that comes across as just slightly condescending.

"Please place it back into the deck...That's a great spot."

"That's a great spot" is unfunny, and also condescending. What's great about an adult putting a card on top of the half-deck in Daryl's hand?

"Now I'll shuffle the cards so even I don't know where it is..."

OK, now assuming this is not the first trick of the day, (and assuming this wasn't meant as a joke—it didn't come across that way) it's been established that Daryl knows his way around a deck of cards. The card is returned where Daryl says it should be placed: on top of the cards in his extended hand. "Now I'll shuffle the cards so even I don't know where it is..." How many intelligent onlookers will swallow that? Fifty percent? Eighty percent? Maybe twenty percent? It's guaranteed not to be as high as we might prefer.

"What was your card? The Three of Clubs? Ladies and gentlemen, the Three of Clubs!"

In the vast universe of trickdom, why choose a routine that requires you to handle the cards in this manner? Many sophisticated onlookers will place this, on my *Hierarchy of Mystery Entertainment,* between Puzzle and Trick. They won't know what's going on, but they will know that Daryl handles the cards differently than they would if they tried to recreate the same plot. They won't know how he got the selected card between the Jacks, and they may not even care, because clearly he does something, ever so slightly (sleightly?) out of the ordinary when the selected card is returned to the cards in his hand.

If your goal is to entertain with *magic*, not with dexterity or flourishes or juggling, stick to the cleanest, strongest effects.

Case Study #3

A Beginner Learns a Classic and Teaches a Lesson.

Kathy Daly serves as the vice president of my firm, Weber Asset Management. She's a woman with a hair-trigger sense of humor and, after working for me "too damn long," a casual interest in magic. Prior to our December, 2002 holiday office party, she asked me to teach her a trick to perform for our colleagues and their spouses. I chose the Invisible Deck (aka the Ultra Mental Deck; it's sold in malls across America, so don't harangue me for "exposing" a classic). Between the dry-aged steaks and the cheesecake, she performed the trick, including all the hackneyed "invisible deck" gags, to a good reaction, and per the normal script when something amazing occurs, one of our group urged her to "Do that again!" Now, in mentoring her, my first and only magic student, I neglected to stress the dictum that my inner twelve-year-old magician now silently bellowed: Never Repeat a Trick!! So in her innocence she completely disregarded centuries of conjuring dogma and she blithely complied. I was appalled, but the train had left the station. She dispensed with the "invisible" deck shtick and simply requested that a card be named, and showed that, yes, that card now was reversed in the deck.

Whoa! The response was stronger than the first time. So naturally, yet another of my loyal staff demanded, "Let *me* name a card!"

"No, No!" I called out over the din of the restaurant. But there was no stopping her now. She was feeling that which turns us on about magic: she was the center of attention, receiving accolades for accomplishing something unfathomable, and she liked the feeling.

And so, for a third (and final) time, she performed the effect, now stripped down to its absolute minimalist presentation, and the reaction, rather than diminishing, grew.

Why? Because the trick is pure. *Name a card. Look, that card is the one card I turned face-down in the deck.* No handling, no suspicious moves. Everything Kathy did was exactly— *exactly*—what she would do if she were to demonstrate this phenomenon for real. Her casual behavior with the cards blocked any suspicion about the deck. No one said, "Let me see those cards!"

* * *

There are a gazillion tricks out there. Ninety percent are crap. That still leaves—what's a gazillion divided by ten?—a supertanker full of direct, powerful tricks. Go find them, and banish everything else.

In the financial world, as Kathy Daly can tell you, investors frequently want to hold onto a down-trodden stock until it gets back to the level they paid for it. But that stock has no memory, nor any emotional attachment to the investor. If it's worth $10,000 today, that's it. Where, the investor must ask, is the best place for that ten grand going forward from today? Likewise, the magician must be coldhearted about his material. Don't marry your stocks, and don't foolishly fall in love with a trick. The investment in a stock or a trick either pays off or it doesn't.

Don't allow your emotions to get in the way of clearheaded decisions about what's best for you.

Look Homeward

Every year, new magic—in the form of tricks, books, and videos—comes hurtling at us at an increasing speed. We have more from which to choose, and much of it is of good quality.

Is that good or bad?

Answer: it's not good. To sum up this chapter on Choosing Material: *stop*!

Stop your treasure hunt (or is it a scavenger hunt?) for your Killer Effect. Whether you bought this book or borrowed it, it's a good bet you're not a beginner in magic. Slow down. Breathe. Focus. If you've been into the mystery arts for even just a few years, your home undoubtedly holds enough books, lecture notes, tricks, and videos to provide a lifetime of fruitful study. You don't need to choose new material from the dealers; you need to rediscover the material that at some point in the past delighted and excited you, and compelled you to make the purchase.

The time you devote to thinking about, and then buying, a new trick is time you are neglecting something you already own. The rush to accumulate new holds back the perfecting of old.

Better to rediscover all the good ideas you have encountered during your travels through the magic world, and which have found a place in the notebook you keep for this purpose.

You do keep a notebook (paper or electronic), don't you?

A Personal Entertainment Highlight:
Del Ray at the Card Table

As with so many in our field, I tend to know of those compatriots who publish or invent, and little of those full-time performers who are out on the road earning a nice living. Somehow, the name Del Ray had escaped my attention, other than being a Florida town down the road from Boca Raton.

That changed when I performed inside a tent at an outdoor fair put on for the employees of a major pharmaceutical company. After my show, I was told that there were fortune-tellers and a magician in another tent, and so I ambled over.

There I saw a quiet, older man holding forth at a large wooden table. At first he seemed to be just another card magician, but what I didn't realize was that I had wandered into the middle of a non-stop four-hour set. Yes, he used cards, but he was doing card tricks I had never seen before. A mechanical bird and other small toy animals appeared and moved around; they were finding selected cards and I quickly realized I had no idea how any of this was happening! Groups of people came over, thoroughly enjoyed his presentations, and then moved on (many attractions were vying for their attention), but I stayed for at least an hour, and don't recall seeing any trick repeated.

All the tricks were done with a playful, understated style that ingratiated every onlooker, none more so than me. I introduced myself during a rare quiet moment, and he was pleasant, but the flow of new ready-to-be-floored spectators never ceased, so I had no opportunity to converse in depth. If he took a break, I never saw it. He seemed to gather in new energy and enthusiasm from each new group, and he never showed the slightest sign of faltering. It was a remarkable display of showmanship, deft technical skills, and joy of performing.

In the years since that day, I learned that, among large segments of the close-up magic community, Del Ray is a legend, and that afternoon made it clear to me why.

Section IV

⋘ PERFORMER ⋙

"One who enacts (a feat or role) before an audience; gives a public presentation."

Chapter 7
Your Appearance

Dress for Success

Whatever style you choose to express, spend some bucks to look good.

Take your cue from Hollywood. Stars look good—even when they shouldn't. In the Hollywood blockbuster film, *Romancing the Stone,* Michael Douglas and Katherine Turner trek across the desert with hair perfectly coiffed. If you give it a moment's thought, it's incredibly silly, but the public likes seeing people who look better than we do in real life.

You are a star when you take the stage. Show me that you respect me (unless you're a rock star—then show me that you don't give a damn about what I think).

Dress appropriately for the occasion. Tuxedos, so common among magicians in the past, now shout "cheesy lounge act" in all but those few occasions where all the other men are similarly attired in penguin-wear. The old rule stands: be the best-dressed person in the room, but don't be overdressed.

Successful corporate magician Bill Malone understands this. According to the October 2002 issue of *Magic* magazine:

"One day," says Bill, "I looked around and saw what these people were driving, the way they were dressed, what kind of jewelry they wore, and I realized right away that it was all kind of a game. If I wanted to play, too, I had to look like they do, so I immediately bought new clothes and stuff. One of the things I needed to fit in was a Rolex, but I didn't have the money for it. So I started giving magic lessons, and I kept giving them until I saved enough to buy one. It was all part of the game."

I agree totally, except about the Rolex. Thanks to my entry into the investment world, I get to pal around with some pretty powerful folks from time to time, and Rolexes, believe it or not,

121

no longer carry the cachet they once did. Just be sure that, whatever timepiece you wear, it sends the message you want.

And if you have to give magic lessons to upgrade your wardrobe, start advertising.

This rule applies regardless of the venues you work. Even if you feel appropriately dressed in a T-shirt and jeans, make sure your T-shirt and jeans are the most upscale ones in the room.

Hands and Nails

A discussion on a magic site discussed the poor appearance of a well-known performer on an instructional video tape:

"I was amazed and SHOCKED to see how chewed-up/ infected/ bruised [the magician's] fingers were. When they came in for the close-ups on the explanations, each hand had at least 2 or more fingers that really looked awful. And this from a guy who works for big bucks doing close-up."

That's just sad—and sadly, not uncommon. Stage performers should have decent looking hands and fingernails, and close-up performers *must* have hands that don't call attention to themselves.

Look at your hands. Do you see anything that might call attention to itself? If you do, remedy the situation. And if you do work close-up, and especially if you work for the "big bucks," be aware that it's becoming less uncommon to see men getting manicures. It could be a good investment—and what a way to meet women!

Shoes

Dull, scuffed shoes can be seen, and will be noted, by more people than you may realize. I have seen performers in tuxedos walk out with scuffed street shoes. That tells the audience, "This is someone who doesn't do the big gigs."

Spend a little extra for top-quality, comfortable shoes that are in style *now*. And keep them polished.

Glasses

If possible, don't wear them. If laser corrective surgery isn't practical or doesn't appeal to you, consider getting contact lenses, at least for your shows if not for full-time use. (I wear one-day disposable contacts, a major breakthrough in convenience for the traveling performer, because you have nothing to carry except the lenses.) Your eyes communicate with the audience, and glasses block or reduce the twinkle in your gaze.

If you must wear glasses:

- Get the most stylish frames you can afford. And remember, styles change every few years. Right now, oversized glasses, once the accessories of the rich and pompous, make you look hopelessly outdated.

- Pay the premium for the thinnest, lightest, most scratch-resistant lenses available. Cheap lenses look cheap; you don't want that.

- An absolute rule for glasses—get *non-reflective coatings* on your lenses. During one of my lectures for the PEA, I literally received gasps from the onlookers when I switched back and forth between glasses with and without the glare-blocking feature. The difference cannot be appreciated until seen, well, eye-to-eye.

- Clean your glasses just before your show.

Handkerchief

Carry one in your back pocket every time you go on stage. Three reasons:

- In your entire career, you may never sneeze on stage, but if you do, whipping out a cotton handkerchief looks much classier than using your sleeve.

- You handle props, and props can chip or splinter and make you bleed. Again, a handkerchief beats your clothing for sopping up body fluids.

- Most important, as the old commercial used to say, "Never let them see you sweat."

123

And you will sweat. You sweat because you're nervous, because you're moving around, and because you're under lights. Stage lights bake performers (recall that fast-food restaurants keep their McGlops warm under lights that look suspiciously similar to stage lights). Use your handy 100% cotton handkerchief to pat yourself dry. It's not a pleasant topic, but I would rather see a performer use the hanky than drip perspiration on the stage, his props, or (yuk) his volunteers.

Your Jacket

Button your jacket before you walk out.

You can open it later in the show, but start out looking your best. A suit jacket—and especially a double-breasted jacket—flopping around when you walk to the center of the stage signals "I'm not all that concerned about being here." (The open double-breasted jacket doesn't seem to bother David Letterman, but you don't have a nightly network talk show.)

Your Shirt

Aside from reminding you to wear a clean, pressed, in-style shirt that goes with the rest of your outfit, there's only one thing to know about shirts:

Never wear a short-sleeved shirt with a jacket! It is acceptable to wear a short-sleeved shirt with a jacket only if you are a NASA engineer, a high school math teacher, or a member of those few other professions for whom the description "nerd" is taken as a compliment.

If it's unbearably hot, take your jacket off *after* you begin.

Chapter 8

Your Voice

"My formula for success? Rise early, work late, strike oil."

Jean Paul Getty

Yes, J. P., luck plays a considerable role in the success of a performer. For just one example, where your Mum happened to pop you out and grow you up makes a difference, because you will sound like your neighbors. That may be fortuitus, or it may be unfortunate. Some of us have naturally pleasing voices, some don't.

An off-putting accent, a whiny voice, a too-slow or too-fast speech pattern: all present obstacles that must first be recognized and then modified. Careful analysis of your videotaped presentation is, again, the first step.

My Favorite Voice Trick

Here's an exercise to illustrate a supremely practical and important technique I learned back in my speech-major days.

We'll use words that appeared in John Northern Hilliard's book, *Greater Magic*. Below you'll see a lightly-edited version of a script for the trick "The Problem Of the Three Coins," which, as Hilliard writes, is "exactly as presented by the well-known mentalist 'Mahendra,' who in private life is Mr. Frank B. Sterling."

Read the following paragraph (don't be concerned with the content or grammar; this is apparently what played well in the 1930s and '40s). Then read it again, out loud. Make an effort to hear yourself as you speak and try to remember what you heard.

Being a mentalist, you expect me to read your minds. Of course, I make no pretension to supernatural power and I do not claim actually to read your mind UNLESS I can get your mind thinking along the lines I wish. In other words, I must make your mind susceptible to my own mental impulses. For example, ask me to tell you what you are thinking of at this moment and I cannot tell you. No person can do that. Anyone who tells you he can read

*your mind, under such circumstances, is a fraud. I do not
say it never will be done. BUT, if you think along certain
lines it is true that I may be able to reveal your thoughts.
To do this, I shall use what psychologists call the principle
of associated thought ideas. Perhaps the simplest form of
the experiment is with money. People have no trouble in
associating ideas with money.*

Finished reading? (You took the lazy way out and didn't
really read it a second time, aloud, did you? See that? I *am* a
mentalist!) Whether you truly read the lines out loud, or just to
yourself, chances are you paused at the commas and periods,
just as you were taught to do in elementary school. That's fine
for everyday life, but not so fine for the entertainer. Our goal is
to stand apart from the ordinary, and to be more interesting
than the average Joe. You increase your audience's interest in
your spoken words by using that great tip I picked up in college:
Ignore Punctuation!

Ignoring most of the punctuation provides two benefits: first,
it makes you sound more natural, more conversational. No
human converses with friends in perfectly punctuated sentences
and paragraphs. Your spectators are your friends—or will soon
become your friends, we hope. If you speak the way you were
taught to read aloud, you will not sound natural; you will sound
as though you are reading.

Second, by inserting unexpected pauses, you break the
normal patterns people expect, and that simple ruse makes you
more interesting. Predictability is poison! Predictability in
anything we do becomes boring. As entertainers, we seek to
continually surprise our viewers, in ways big and small, and
changing expected speech patterns is one small way to help
maintain interest.

I don't know whether they do it consciously or not, but I can
tell you that all leading news broadcasters ignore punctuation
as they recite the words they read off the TelePrompTer. Not
with every sentence, but most. Prove it to yourself by listening
to them and picturing the written sentences as they speak. And
certainly, actors learn to speak in a manner that sounds like
real-life speech.

Now let's get to the type of exercise I was taught when I was a speech/drama major in college. Below you will find the same patter, but this time presented with a different speech pattern, brought about by ignoring much of the written punctuation.

Some points to keep in mind as you read it:

- These may not be the pauses that fit *your* style. They work for me, but only trial and error will produce the correct comfort level for you.

- You may find it difficult to say these lines as you see them here. That's to be expected. It takes some work. *It's called rehearsal.* You will not feel comfortable doing it at first (if you prefer, think of this exercise as learning a new sleight!).

- Many of the pauses, as indicated by the line breaks, will be quick, almost imperceptible, perhaps accompanied by a tilt of the head, a raised brow, a hand gesture, or an inhalation.

- And remember, this is only a learning exercise to help you break lifelong patterns. These are not your words; they are someone else's words for a routine you will probably never perform. Forget about the actual words; just go with the flow of it, and have fun with it.

After you read through it once or twice, proceed to the next section where you will learn the next, equally important step in this technique.

Being a mentalist, you expect me to
read your minds.
Of course, I make no pretension
to supernatural power
and I do not claim actually to read your mind
UNLESS I can get your mind thinking
along the lines I wish. In other words,
I must make your mind susceptible to
my own
mental impulses. For example,
ask me to tell you what you are thinking of
at this moment and

I cannot tell you. No person can do that.
Anyone who tells you
he can read your mind, under such circumstances,
is a fraud.
I do not say it never will be done.
BUT, if you think along certain lines
it is true that I
may be able to reveal your thoughts. To do this,
I shall use what psychologists call the
principle of associated
thought
ideas.
Perhaps the simplest form of the experiment is with
money.
People have no trouble in associating ideas with
money.

After you've decided where your pauses will be, your next step is to decide where you are going to vocally add emphasis. Don't do this in your head; *mark the relevant places on your script.* Take out a pencil and underline what you think are the key words. Then read it aloud, after which you will undoubtedly make changes.

Do not skip this vital step. By consciously calling your attention to specific words in your script, you reduce the need to think about "showmanship" later on. The underlines, you will find, do the thinking for you.

Being a mentalist, you _expect_ *me to*
read your minds.
Of course, I make no _pretension_
to supernatural power
and I do not claim _actually_ *to read your mind*
UNLESS I can get your mind thinking
along the lines I wish. In other words,
I must make _your_ *mind susceptible to*
my _own_

*mental impulses. For example,
ask me to tell you what you are <u>thinking</u> of
at this moment and
I <u>cannot</u> tell you. No person can do that.
Anyone who tells you
he can read your mind, under such circumstances,
is a <u>fraud</u>.
I do not say it <u>never</u> will be done.
BUT if you think along certain lines
it is true that I
<u>may</u> be able to reveal your thoughts. To <u>do</u> this,
I shall use what psychologists call the
principle of associated
thought
ideas.
Perhaps the <u>simplest</u> form of the experiment is with
money.
People have <u>no</u> trouble in associating ideas with
money.*

Finally, you put it all down in a condensed format, using slashes (/) or ellipses (...) to indicate your own personalized punctuation.

Being a mentalist, you <u>expect</u> me to ... read your minds...Of course, I make no <u>pretension</u> ...to supernatural power ...and I do not claim <u>actually</u> to read your mind ...<u>UNLESS</u> I can get your mind thinking ...along the lines I wish In other words ...I must make <u>your</u> mind susceptible to ... my <u>own</u> ... mental impulses For example, ... ask me to tell you what you are <u>thinking</u> of ... at this moment and ... I <u>cannot</u> tell you No person can do that ...Anyone who tells you ... he can read your mind, under such circumstances ... is a <u>fraud</u> ... I do not say it <u>never</u> will be done ... BUT... if you think along certain lines ... it is true that I ... <u>may</u> be able to reveal your thoughts To <u>do</u>

129

this ... I shall use what psychologists call the ... principle ... of associated ... thought ... ideas... Perhaps the simplest form of the experiment is with ... money. ... People have no trouble in associating ideas with ... money.

Again, this is a learning exercise, one which is difficult to translate onto paper, and it probably did not feel comfortable for you. (I don't remember specifically, but I imagine it felt equally strange to me when I was taught this technique back at Hofstra University.) It *will* feel much more comfortable when the words are your own. What I can tell you with certainty is that this works for me, powerfully.

Change the Em-**pha**-sis to a Different Syl-**la**-ble

Closely aligned with the above exercise, *Ignore Punctuation*, is *Change the Emphasis*.

This is the technique I use to keep myself sounding fresh and in the moment. Some sections of my show contain words I have said, in exactly the same order, hundreds of times. Consciously varying the placement of the pauses and, particularly, of the emphasized words, forces me to stay alert. I don't lapse into a mental sluggishness, a common malady of successful performers who say the same thing night after night after night.

To demonstrate, we'll use a chunk of patter from Chuck Hickok's eminently practical book, *Mentalism, Incorporated.* These are his opening lines (if ever words are subject to the dreariness of repetition, it's our opening lines). Below you will see three versions of these two short sentences, each with the emphasis placed in different spots. In all three cases, you "say" the same thing, yet each delivers a slightly different message to the listeners.

I'm delighted to be here today and have the opportunity to talk about and demonstrate some untapped powers of the human mind. My interest in the untapped powers of the mind can be traced back to something that happened to me on the day of my tenth birthday.

I'm delighted to be <u>here</u> today and have the opportunity to talk about <u>and</u> demonstrate some untapped <u>powers</u> of the human mind. My <u>interest</u> in the <u>untapped</u> powers of the mind can be traced <u>back</u> to something that happened to me on the day of my <u>tenth</u> birthday.

I'm delighted to be here <u>today</u> and have the <u>opportunity</u> to talk about and <u>demonstrate</u> some untapped powers of the human <u>mind</u>. My interest in the untapped <u>powers</u> of the mind can be traced back to <u>something</u> that happened to me on the day of my tenth <u>birthday</u>.

If you don't perform on a regular basis you may not appreciate the importance of this technique. But for those who sometimes feel they must grind out "another" show, this skill is invaluable for keeping your presentation garden-fresh.

Talk in Color, Not Black and White

When you view your video of yourself, what do you hear? Is your voice as flat as the road from Enid, Oklahoma, to Paris, Texas? Or do your listeners get to enjoy some interesting verbal scenery, with undulating twists and dips?

If you speak anytime during your performance, your voice must be considered with at least as much gravitas as any move, feint, or prop. Fortunately, you don't need to purchase an expensive book of secrets from a magic shop to learn how to turn your voice into the effective communication tool it must become. Help surrounds you. Just start listening analytically to professional speakers.

One of the best sources for inspiration is the HBO TV show, *Def Poetry.* If you think poetry is a singsong recitation of rhyming lines or dry, dense phrases filled with obscure references, you've never seen this powerful show. The mostly young poets spew rage and humor, sarcasm and sensuality, history and contemporary issues with rarely matched passion and vocal intensity.

Using only their voices and, to a lesser degree, their bodies, they communicate an astounding range of emotion and personal, bottom-of-my-soul information. Watch them and learn the power of the spoken word.

Though you may never approach the oral fervor of the *Def Poets* (I actually cannot imagine any magician or mentalist sounding like them but, then, I never could have imagined a David Blaine), still your goal is to vary your:

- pitch
- tone
- volume
- pacing

An entertainer's voice needs color. Watching old-fashioned black-and-white television broadcasts was fine until color came along and we realized that was (usually) better. A college lecturer's voice needs merely to deliver information: the black-and-white picture. You are a delivery system for full rainbow-spectrum emotion.

As you view your video, look for opportunities where you can inject your warmth, turn up the vocal intensity, pause for emphasis, lower the volume for dramatic effect, or otherwise use your voice to raise the impact level of your effects.

And for my younger readers, *please* avoid the Valley Girl syndrome that has infected so much of a generation—the rising inflection at the end of a sentence. Because that's, like, ineffective? And, you know, not a persuasive way of, like, talking?

Hear the Voices

Finally, open yourself up to inspiration. It's everywhere, freely available and close at hand. At your local library, haunt the books-on-tape section and learn why authors like Stephen King and John Grisham demand that certain voice talent be featured when their books are turned into performances. You'll learn to recognize some of the hardest-working voices in the field of books-on-tape entertainment. Check out the work of readers such as Michael Beck, who's read close to a dozen of John Grisham's novels for the audio-book trade, and Frank Muller, who's done the same for Stephen King. While you're listening, ask yourself what makes these readers so successful, their work so compelling, with nothing more than an author's words and their voices? Once you begin doing this, you'll be well on your way to taking your voice seriously.

Chapter 9
Language Skills

You are a writer. Even if you ignore the advice in the chapter on Scripting and even if you never commit your words to paper or computer screen, as long as you speak to your audience with pre-planned words, you are a writer.

Writing is mind-to-mind communication. You, the entertainer, send your thoughts out through your mouth, whereas the novelist types them for readers to read. In both cases, entertainer and writer, one mind seeks to connect with another.

The professional writer knows that every word counts. Excess words allow minds to wander. The professional writer crafts his words, and then an editor refines and polishes. Entertainers rarely have a director, let alone the luxury of an editor.

Writing is easy; good writing is hard. I know that to be true from tortured experience. For ten years I wrote an investment newsletter, *Weber's Fund Advisor*, and I received laudatory letters saying my publication was one of the better-written financial services. *If* that was true, it was more a reflection of the sad state of financial newsletters than on any reportorial skills I possessed. I always felt that whatever meager writing talent I exhibited stemmed from my being a good *reader*, and I kept re-writing my eight-page newsletter (which contained mostly charts and graphs) until what I read no longer embarrassed me.

As entertainers, we must write clearly. Before anything else can happen, our audience must know what we mean. That's why you must relentlessly drive yourself to fashion your words with precision.

Words and Phrases We Can Do Without

Every word you utter has impact, so you must strive to eliminate words that add nothing—or worse, tarnish your aura. Here are a few common examples:

- Magicians and mentalists perennially begin effects by announcing, "Let's **try** something." "Let's **try** an experiment." "Let's **try**..."

The word "try" and its siblings—attempt, endeavor, take a shot, take a stab—are weak, flaccid words. Think back to "The Empire Strikes Back," when Yoda forcefully directs Luke Skywaker to "Do or do not. There is no *try*."

Yes, in some cases you do want to hedge your bet and "try" allows that. And it may be brought into play to boost tension, by implying that this may work for you tonight, or it might not. You are saying to your audience, in effect, "I sure hope you're here on one of those good nights when this works!" (Escape artists thrive by casting doubt on the outcome.) So if you *want* to play that note, use it. Just be sure you're not using it because that's the way it was written in the instructions for the trick.

English performer Derren Brown uses "try" several times on his TV specials. It plays well for him because he works so strongly that he actually needs to throw some uncertainty into the mix, if for no other reason than to vary the tension level. When he says he wants to *try* something, you get the feeling that this may well be the moment when you will see him fail. The same holds true for many mentalists who give the impression that each "experiment" they do (and I'm not a fan of "experiment" either) is something where the outcome is in doubt.

For most other performers, including almost every magician, the audience has little or no doubt that they will succeed, so the "try" becomes superfluous at best, and because your audience may feel an undercurrent of unnecessary verbal deception, it may start to sound as insincere as it in fact is.

- A silk (or polyester) cloth is not a "**silk**." It might be a cloth, a piece of cloth, a silk cloth, a bandana, or a kerchief, but the term "silk" is not used by normal folk.
- "Say 'Stop' as I **riffle** through the cards." When did you ever hear a non-magician use the word riffle? They don't. You might "flip" through the cards. Or you could just ask your participant to, "Say 'Stop' as I go through the cards."
- "Here's a **bit** you may enjoy." A "bit" connotes lower-end show biz. At least say, "Here's something you may enjoy."

- Show normal people the cube we call a **die**. Ask what you're holding and they will say a "dice." Our "die" may be correct English, but it is not commonly known. You might say with a friendly smile, "two dice, one die," to avoid confusion.

- **"For my first trick..."** Why would you say something so obvious? Ditto for **"For my next trick..."**

- "For my next **effect**" is worse still. What, to a layperson, is an *effect*? It's a meaningless filler word that takes you nowhere. (Ricky Jay repeatedly used the word "effect" in his show, *Ricky Jay and His 52 Assistants*. However, in that context it fit because he was giving, in essence, a history lesson about magic, and so it affected the desired effect.)

- **"Just like that."** As in, "And I threw the coins into the invisible hole, just... like... that." Tedious, meaningless, and when repeated more than once, boring. If I can see what you just did, it's redundant to tell me you did it "just like that." Or "Place your hand on the cards, just like that," which sounds patronizing.

- And when the spectator does as asked, the "just like that" is often followed, enthusiastically, with either **"Great!"** or worse, **"That's fantastic!"** (British performers substitute **"Brilliant!"**)

Unless you're going for a laugh, when you bray "Fantastic!" or "Wonderful!" or "Brilliant!" to a spectator upon completion of a simple request, you have just told that person that you assumed her incapable of following your instructions. And the more enthusiastic you are, the more explicit your message becomes.

If you must indicate that the person has done what you want, think of other ways to signal your satisfaction, without demeaning them. Perhaps a simple "Thanks" or just a quick "Perfect," said as an aside.

- **"Just so."** As in, "I'll place these cards over here, just so." Again, it adds nothing; it's just so much filler.

- **"Would you like to change your mind?"** is a cliché, and come hell or high water, clichés should be avoided like the plague. It can also seem slightly insulting to participants, suggesting that their original choices were poor ones, or that they're incapable of making good choices the first time. Be more specific about the options for changing their *decision*. "Should I continue dropping cards?" Or, "I'm going to offer you one last chance to choose a different envelope. Do you want the one you have, or one of these in my hand?" These phrases have more power than "Do you want to change your mind?" or any of its variations.

- **"Are you sure?"** In my life, I'm "sure" about my love of family, I'm sure that I never want to miss my return flight home, and I'm certain that I want the stock market to move higher over the long-term. Those are things about which I'm sure. Now you come along, offer me a choice of five cards (or meaningless—to me—symbols, colors, or envelopes) and then, when I point to one, you ask me if I'm "sure." Sure about what? Are there dire consequences awaiting me if I choose poorly? How carefully should I consider my options? After all, as far as I can tell, the only thing at risk is *your* smug satisfaction! Again, it's meaningless magic-speak filler. Most often, it's best to simply accept the spectator's judgment and proceed. Or, if you do have a legitimate desire to build up the suspense, use specifics: "Later tonight, you may think back on this moment and wonder if I influenced you with my hands or voice, so I'll wait quietly while you decide."

- **"What made you choose...?"** In the countless times I have seen magicians and mentalists ask this question ("What made you choose the circle?"), have I ever heard an interesting response? Not that I can recall. Again—as with "Are you sure?"—it's silly filler that confounds spectators. Either don't ask, or add something new, as in, "The circle is typically chosen by sex-starved alcohol abusers." *Now* you can ask, "Are you sure you want the circle?"

- **"What's the name of your card?"** That phrase, used by every magician at some time in his life, has little meaning for some laymen. I have seen, just during the time I've been writing this book, spectators look confused when asked this question. Cards do not have names, unless you're doing one of the tricks that exploit this phrase (the Fred/Phil Trick). "Which card did you select?" is the better question.

- Kreskin says **"no way, shape, or form,"** way too often. It's a bloated phrase, but many mentalists and magicians picked up on it and now use it as well.

- Any variation of **"Let me show you the first trick I learned."** In the brief time I'll be watching you, I don't want to see what you did as a kid, a beginner. I want to see the tricks that took you years to master. Would a theatrical agent, who has the moral authority to request something specific from you, ask to see your first trick? No, she wants to see your best stuff. The audience can't and won't ask you, but they too want your best. Don't make them feel cheated.

   Of course, you *could* perform your first trick if you preface it with something dramatic, for example, "This was taught to me by a famous magician who made me *swear* to keep it a secret!" You could say that... if you can say it with conviction because it's reasonably true.

- **"What I'm going to do now..."** or **"What I'd like you to do..."** or **"What I need you to do..."** Skip it. Can it. Drop it. Just get to the point.

- **"Alright?"** Nervous magicians follow every action with this word (which is technically an incorrect version of "all right," but we're dealing with spoken English here). "You can see the cards are well mixed, alright?" "I'll place each card in an envelope, alright?" Are those nervous-nellies waiting for a response? I hope not.

- Or its variation, **Right?** "I'm going to roll this newspaper into a cone... Right?" The first time I saw myself on tape, it seemed every fifth word I said was "Right?"

- **"...and with any luck**, the final coin will now have joined the others." As Tina Turner might say, "What's luck got to do with it?" It's another stale phrase that we use without thinking—one which, if we do give it some thought, implies we're not in control of the magic.

- **"You've been a great crowd."** A vastly overused cliché, thanks to stand-up comics. Think of other ways to express your appreciation to your audience.

- Any variation of **"Is that fair?"** as in, "and now I'll let you cut the cards as many times as you wish. Is that fair?" This immediately sets up a challenge; you have now told me that I must evaluate whether what you just did is "fair" or not. Fair how? By what standards? Fair to whom? And most important, *why should I care?* What's in it for me if what you do is fair, or... what? Unfair? Much better to be specific, as cited above in, "Would you like to change your mind?"

    The obvious exception to this is when you are in fact laying down a challenge, as in an escape act or when doing what mentalists call "test-condition" effects.

- **"Now let's make it a little more interesting..."** is usually said to indicate a higher degree of difficulty, or, in a gambling situation, higher stakes. But if you have to announce to me that something is "more interesting," it probably isn't; the words are unadulterated filler. If the next moments truly *are* more interesting, you should trust that your spectators possess sufficient brainpower to realize that for themselves. Tell me specifics about what's coming next, not banal generalities.

- **"And for those of you in the cheap seats..."** This phrase had mold growing on it when vaudeville was young. David Copperfield can legitimately refer to cheap seats (or at least, cheaper seats); few of the rest of us can. Use this phrase and some people will laugh, but many others will recognize you as a person who belongs in the cheap seats yourself. Plus, think about it—if you actually did have different seat prices and you made that "joke," how did you just make those who couldn't afford the better seats feel?

    At a major magic convention in 2003 I heard a well-known (among magicians) performer use this phrase twice in one short set. Get with the new millennium!

Back to Grammar School

Whether we care to admit it or not, people judge us by our outward appearance and by the way we speak. Everyone, no matter how erudite, slips occasionally and says something that may be considered wordy, redundant, or pretentious. Then there's grammar. Among some in your audience, poor grammar leads to an immediate "ouch," the same way as a palmed card inadvertently flashed. You are judged by your use of the language, so you want to keep errors to a minimum.

Just a few samples of less-than-stellar language skills I've recently heard from the mouths of performers:

"At this point in time..." should be "at this point" or "at this time" or simply "now."

"Could care less" is careless English. When you reach absolute zero emotional attachment to any particular subject you are in a state where you "could *not* care less." To say you *could* care less means that you *do* have feelings, exactly the opposite of what you want to convey.

"Irregardless..." No such word, regardless of what you may think.

"Should have went...", *"Could have wrote..."* Have gone. Have written.

"Her/Him and I..." She/He and I.

"Between you and I..." Between you and me.

If you have any fear that your grasp of English may lead to muffled chuckles among your spectators, ask a knowledgeable friend to watch your videotape to check for verbal flubs. (Columnist William Safire, self-described "language maven" for the *New York Times Sunday Magazine*, bravely includes corrections lobbed at him by what he calls the Gotcha! Squad. Now that I've written this section, I too must brace for the inevitable repercussions. Fair enough. Him and me must eat what we kills.)

Honesty is the Best Policy

Magicians lie. Your Egg Bag really isn't empty; you do in fact know which card was selected; the solid steel rings aren't quite as they appear.

So why lie any more than you must? Don't tell me about a funny thing that happened on the way to the show tonight if it never happened. I don't want to hear that, "the other day a guy said, 'Yeah, but can I see what's *under* the hat'," if no such guy crossed your path recently. Magicians constantly throw in these trivial lines and the lines invariably ring false. Save for the occasional accomplished actor among us, the audience knows you're fibbing, and it cheapens the moment.

Unless you're going for a strong punch line, the best policy is to be as truthful as possible.

You can, of course, delve into a richly detailed narrative, one speckled with fictionalized moments, which serves to Communicate Your Humanity or perhaps to deliver Rapt Attention. But again, that's territory for those elite few who can convincingly enthrall us with words. The art of skillful lying (which might be better termed, "acting") develops over years, and you'd be wise to approach it slowly and cautiously.

And please, if you promise something, don't welch on that promise.

Here's a minor example: it's from Bill Malone's four-video collection, *"On The Loose,"* which I consider to be high school, college, and graduate work on how to present a solid set of thoroughly entertaining close-up card magic. Toward the beginning of his terrific Three Card Monte routine, he says, "and when I'm done I'll teach everyone how the trick works. OK? Is that a deal?"

But he doesn't truly teach it, and at the end, sure enough, the spectator who served as the "victim" says, during the applause, "I thought you were going to show me how to do it!"

"Yeah, I was..." Bill says with a sly smirk to the audience.

Many of us have done things like that. We don't need it. Let's stop.

Raising Hands

"How many of you enjoy mystery novels?"

"How many of you like eating at fine restaurants?"

There is a virus spreading among corporate and motivational speakers, and now some magicians and mentalists are infected as well. It's the mindless asking for a show of hands. I find it patronizing and annoying.

Don't ask me something if the answer doesn't truly matter to you.

Some performers fall back on these questions because they think it's a form of audience participation, when in reality it's the same as bread crumbs in cheap crab cakes: filler. Your audience craves sustenance, not filler.

There are legitimate reasons to poll your audience. Perhaps you truly do need to learn something about who is out there looking at you (although it's usually too late to be doing research once you're standing on stage).

Or you may be using the "How many of you...?" query as the setup for a joke. Israeli magician and mentalist Lior Manor works for major corporations around the world, and he starts his show by saying, "You hear I talk with an accent. So, I can do my act in bad English or perfect Hebrew. How many of you want me to do it in bad English?"

Hands go up, and the audience is smiling immediately.

Say What?

Speakers use an offshoot of "raising hands" that I find equally irritating and useless: the unfinished sentence. They turn to the audience and wait for them to shout out the final word or words.

As in "Many people won't touch frogs because they're afraid of getting ...?"

Or they use a variation on that theme: the sentence ending in "what?"

"Money is printed by governments so that we can have... what?"

I rarely see magicians do this, but I have seen mentalists and hypnotists employ this strategy. It's dumb for two reasons:

- If everyone knows the answer, why did you bother asking? It didn't move the program along; it slowed it down.

- If most people don't know the answer to your query, suddenly we're back in school and some of us feel dumb. Thanks for that! I have a wife and kids to remind me of my mental frailty; I don't need some stranger rubbing it in.

Closely related to the Say What? and Raising Hands annoyances are the many performers who ask their audience for permission, as in, "Now we're going to play a little lottery game...is that OK with everybody?" And then they wait for a response.

Wimpy! Superman controls every moment.

Every time you ask an audience anything, and then pause for a response, you momentarily cede control. Be certain you have a clear and compelling reason for your query. Again, what reaction are you targeting? If it's not laughter or rapt attention, your show will be better without it.

Don't State the Obvious!

When watching a performer, nothing bores me faster than his telling me something I already know. Don't mention that the sky is blue, that women are more emotional than men, and don't ever tell me, "I have here a deck of cards."

Why are you telling me that? Do I not have eyes to see?

You tell me what you "have here" only when it's something I would not easily recognize, as in "I have here a miniature Egyptian sarcophagus, exhumed from deep below the Museum Store at the Roosevelt Field Mall."

Similarly, during the show don't tell me what you are doing or about to do.

"Now I'll cut the rope in the middle."

"I'm going to shuffle the cards."

"I'll just place the lid back on the pan."

Boring! Adults don't need to be told the obvious. So unless you're a kids' show entertainer, just do the action, or come up with words that add something to the moment.

And only for the sake of completeness am I bringing up the Magic 101 advice about, "This is an ordinary deck of cards." Never refer to any prop as "ordinary." A deck of cards, a coin, a pad of paper, a piece of rope are all presumed to be ordinary, unless you raise suspicion or needlessly draw attention to them.

All overtly magical props are assumed to be suspect and can never be labeled as "ordinary" (I pray that no one has ever uttered the words, "I have here an ordinary Zig-Zag box").

Chapter 10
How to Be Funny!

In *The Producers*, the Mel Brooks film and blockbuster Broadway show of the same name, the plot revolves around a scheme to cash in handsomely from a sure-fire flop (what else could *Springtime for Hitler* possibly be?). If you, dear reader, can figure out a way to show a profit from an act that goes down the commode, here's my guaranteed formula for your success... I mean, failure:

Early in your act, tell a joke, preferably a weak joke, one that you've never before told in public. When you get to the last word of the joke, stop, smile, and stand there, waiting for the laugh.

Repeat.

Then, when you are ready to do some magic, change the pace by saying, "But seriously, folks..."

The sound you will hear at this point is the nervous shifting of audience members in their seats. Do not let that distract you. Your rags-to-riches death-spiral will be gaining momentum.

On the other hand...

You may prefer jokes that trigger laughter, not groans. If that's the case, let's steal a lesson from two of America's best-known comedians. Each weekday night, David Letterman and Jay Leno face the daunting task of finding the yuks in the daily headlines.

Look at how they typically handle new material—and of course, in their cases, the monologues not only have never been audience-tested, the jokes may have been reworked up until minutes before being delivered into the bedrooms of millions of late-night viewers.

Dave and Jay both *talk through* the punch line. That is, when they arrive at the final word of the joke, they often tack on a few additional words (an example, from Letterman: "It was so hot today... on my walk through Central Park this morning I saw a squirrel moisturizing his nuts... it was just that hot!").

Nonetheless, when saying something funny, *wait for the laugh* before moving on to the next thought (the "talk-through"

145

technique extends the *current* thought). I recently watched a tape of a performance I gave for the Psychic Entertainers Association in 2001. It was the opening night of the three-day convention, and that day, a Thursday, historically has been, shall we say, a bit "looser" than the more formal Friday and Saturday night shows, which are open to the public. My presentation consisted of two routines prepared solely for that night—in other words, never seen before, and never to be seen again, and marbled nicely, or so I thought, with big just-for-the-guys laugh lines. Well, I tell you, dammit, they *were* funny, but in my nervousness (there's nothing harder than performing new material for peers) I raced right through almost every punch line, moving from one new thought to another.

If only I had written this book a couple of years ago, I might have saved my sorry ass that night! Learn from my mistakes.

The Two Hooks for Humor

All humor in magic and mentalism acts falls into two categories:

- funny moments that emanate organically from the situation *This is by far the superior choice.*
- funny moments meant to stand on their own, apart from the miraculous things we do (in other words, jokes or other "gags")

First, let's examine choice number one, which can itself be divided in two. First up is the natural outcome to what we do, the humor that spontaneously springs from the moment of surprise: the *Eek!* Moment. Because that surprise is wrapped in a non-threatening blanket of supportive fun, the release almost always manifests itself as laughter. When a woman finds an overflowing warren of sponge rabbits in her hand when she expected only two, her surprise turns into laughs, and onlookers laugh with her. Remove a bowling ball from a shopping bag, no one laughs. Remove it from a thin briefcase—that's funny! Put a beer bottle into a paper bag, then suddenly crush the bag—we laugh.

Among performing artists, only magicians can lay claim to these unexpected, startling moments of delight. Not every trick evokes laughter, but many do, especially when there's a visual non sequitur (a bowling ball from a thin case).

In addition to the shock of the climax, the best humor in magical situations comes from the unusualness of the situation ("You want me to burn the envelope with the money inside?") or the tension of the moment just prior to the climax (as when the spectator says "If I'm holding the silver coin now, I'll scream!").

The second type of humor for us is the intentional use of words to raise a smile, and here is where we get into trouble.

If you tell jokes of any kind, and they are not intrinsic to the trick, *you'd better be certain they are of comedy club caliber.* Make that *contemporary* comedy club caliber. Henny Youngman and Jack Carter yukked it up on *The Ed Sullivan Show* with mother-in-law jokes. You can't do that, even if your mother-in-law *does* wax her moustache.

We now live in a time when almost any town large enough for an airport has a comedy club, and the Comedy Central TV channel beams buckets of cutting-edge clowning into millions of homes across the United States. Audiences know new from old, clever from pedestrian, and if you're smart, you won't take on the comedy pros at their own game, unless you're sure you can.

It's much better to find the fun in the situation. We have an advantage over comedians: we do amazing things, *and* we can talk. They talk, but they don't do amazing things.

Unfortunately, some of our top pros muddle their entertainment message.

Turning again to Bill Malone's *On the Loose*, we see even this top-ranked professional throw in a few "jokes" that don't fit the spontaneous feel of the balance of the program. (To a female spectator, "You would look good in 3D... that's my room at the Hyatt." To a male spectator, "What do you do for a living? ... Oh, OK, I'll talk slower.") He doesn't need those jokes at all; yes, they get laughs, but I don't think it's worth the price (admittedly small) he pays. To me, they momentarily jar the mood and detract from his image as Superman with a deck of

147

cards. The strong magic itself, and his effervescent personality, produce a feeling of non-stop fun. He doesn't need—and chances are *you* don't need—what many in the audience will recognize as canned "zingers."

When you do kick-to-the-head, entertaining magic (as Bill Malone does), have faith in the magic and the humor inherent in the magic.

All the best comedy moments in magic—*every one*—come from the magic itself or the situation around the magic.

My advice: script your routines with nary a "joke" in sight. Once you begin performing the trick, the humor will rise to the surface on its own, and then you work those naturally occurring laughs into your performance. This is especially important if you are not a naturally funny person.

In my own case, after having done thousands of successful shows, I know I can make audiences laugh. But I learned early on to chuck all my crafty one-liners and let the magic—or even better, the spectators—get the laughs.

If you have any sense of humor at all, funny lines *will* pop out of you from time to time during performances, or one of your spectators will spout a few words that produce a laugh. After the show, make an effort to recall the spontaneously comic moments, and *write them down.*

I never did enough of this. I would fire off some clever remark, one that perfectly fit the moment, and during the ensuing laugh I would say to myself, "Well, *that's* staying in the show!" It was so perfect, there was no way I could possibly forget it. Except that too often, I did. In the chapter called *After the Show,* I'll remind you about the importance of consciously making the effort to recall—and record—the ad-libs and funny moments that worked.

Get to the Point... Quickly

In the literature for high-end audio equipment, the term "listener fatigue" refers to the tendency of cheaper equipment to reduce the enjoyment of music over the course of thirty to sixty minutes. The effect, subtle and subconscious, has been studied and documented. A similar phenomenon takes place over the course of your performance. Bloated sentences and puffy punch-lines fatigue the audience.

Danny Orleans, in his *Genii* column on performing for kids, once wrote about the *economy of words* necessary for successful jokes. Whether for four-year old kids or bent-over seniors, the principle stands: *unnecessary words blunt the humor.*

Danny offers an example: in setting up the situation for the Break-away Fan, he chooses a girl with long hair. When showing that the fan "works," he fans toward the girl's face and her hair flies up. That gets a laugh. Then he repeats the bit somewhat differently, producing another laugh. Finally, he turns to the little boy on his other side and says, "Watch out... her hair wiggles!"

And those *five* words get a big laugh.

The way Danny describes the routine leaves no doubt that any adults watching would be laughing along with the children. Danny points out that *wiggles* is a funny word; saying her hair *moves* or *flies up* would not be the same. Equally important, the joke is reduced to the essential words.

A less experienced performer might say to the boy, "Did you notice? Every time I do this, her hair goes flying up in the air?" That would also would produce laughs, but fewer.

In humor, almost always, less is more.

Here's a joke I saw on the Internet. First, you'll see it exactly as it appeared, in what I would call the Corporate Speaker version:

Every Friday afternoon, a mathematician/physicist goes to a bar. He sits in the second-to-last seat and turns to the last seat—which is always empty—and asks a girl—who isn't there—if he can buy her a drink.

The bartender, who is used to weird university types, shrugs but keeps quiet. However, when Valentine's Day arrives, and the mathematician makes a particularly heart-wrenching plea into empty space, and his curiosity gets the better of the bartender. He says, "I apologize if this strikes you as a stupid question, but surely you know there is never a woman sitting in that last stool. Why do you persist in asking out someone who's not even there?"

The university nerd replies, "Well, according to quantum physics, empty space is never truly empty. Virtual particles come into existence and vanish all the time. You never know when the proper wave function will implode and a girl might suddenly appear there."

The bartender raises his eyebrows. "Really? Interesting. But couldn't you just ask one of the girls who comes here every Friday if you could buy her a drink? You never know... she might say yes."

The nerd laughs. "Yeah, right... like that could happen!"

Now, the more professional, condensed version:

Every Friday a physicist goes to a bar, turns to the empty seat next to him, and asks an imaginary girl if he can buy her a drink.

He does this for months.

Finally the bartender says, "You know, there's never a woman sitting next to you. Why do you keep asking out someone who's not even there?"

The physicist says, "Well, according to quantum physics, empty space is never truly empty. You never know when the proper wave function will implode and a girl might suddenly appear there."

The bartender says, "Oka-a-y. But couldn't you ask one of the girls who comes here if you could buy her a drink? She might say yes."

The nerd laughs. "Yeah, right... like that could happen!"

That's 202 words vs. 124 words. It's the same joke, but without the potential for listener fatigue created by all the excess verbiage.

As Shakespeare told us, "Brevity is the soul of wit."

Use Humor with Compassion

Sarcasm works for the right performer in the right situation—as long as it's light sarcasm. As with habañero pepper sauce, a little goes a long way, and a heavy hand with the sarcasm backfires quickly. Never become hostile, and *never* use humor to strike out at an audience member. Whenever possible, turn your jokes back onto yourself.

What if your joke dies a silent death? Smile, or make a joke about the moment, but *never blame the audience.* Nine times out of ten, those Robert Orben-esque "savers" we've all heard (or used) only dig you into a deeper hole.

Master Your Domain

Jerry Seinfeld's *cinema verité* documentary, *Comedian*, exposes the unfunny work that happens before the laughter. It shows in gritty detail that casually riffing on the foibles of the world may look easy and untailored, but those who successfully do it for a living regularly fall prey to nagging bouts of anxiety and self-doubt. And, importantly for the readers of this book, they approach their work with discipline bordering on fanatical.

A comedian's arsenal consists of words and his body. He has no tricks to hide behind. The words, the delivery, the timing are everything.

While magicians rehearse their moves, comedians rehearse and refine their patter, their presentation in total. They know comedy is delicate: a sneeze in the audience can ruin a laugh line; turning your head this way for a particular joke is funny, and that way it's not. Every gesture, every word assumes great importance.

Are you fanatical about the words you say?

Do you give your patter the same thought and practice that you give your sleights?

If not, why not?

151

A Personal Entertainment Highlight:
Mac King

Mac King? The toothy, country-bumpkin fellow in the used-car-sales-man plaid jacket who teaches low-rent tricks to C-list celebrities on TV magic specials as a bumper between the real "stars" of magic? *That* guy?

Yes, that's what I thought, too, until I saw him perform live at a magic convention. Now I understand why he has a multi-year, multi-million-dollar Las Vegas contract.

Unlike what we saw on TV, his live show flows and builds brilliantly. Various bits and gags continually reappear throughout, each time increasing the laugh value. Fig Newton cookies, as I recall, have nothing to do with anything, but simply keep showing up at inappropriate times (as when the participant has been "trained" to expect her selected card to be in his outside coat pocket, and suddenly there is a Fig Newton; then, when he seems to be finding cards in his fly, what should appear but—another Fig Newton. And so on.). There's never an explanation as to why they keep showing up, which makes the incongruity of it all even funnier. And eventually the card appears inside a small cereal box. All the while he perfectly plays this "nice but none-too-bright guy from Kentucky," letting his personality win over the audience, not to mention the fact that a lot of amazing things happen while he's on stage.

His finale is the production—as a "thank you" gift—of a bottle of beer from a cloth he's been using for something else. Along the way, he also finds stuff in his shoe, including a stone that's slightly larger than the shoe itself!

Naturally, he has an unending supply of perfectly matched "lines" to go with all of this.

I remember leaving his show thinking, "Wow! *This* is what professional comedy magic looks like!"

Section V

"The articles used in a particular activity; equipment."

Chapter 11
Sound and Lighting

For me, the biggest mystery in my beloved craft has nothing to do with sleights, mirrors, or gaffs. Instead, I scratch my head over the unfathomable lack of interest displayed by so many performers regarding the sound and lighting of their shows.

After all, what is your show? They see you. They hear you. There is nothing else! (Smell, touch, and taste rarely make an appearance.)

Your show *is* sight and sound.

If the audience cannot hear your words clearly, if they cannot see your hands, your facial expressions, your volunteers, and your props, all your cleverness and hours of practice count for naught. Why, then, do so many performers in our field—including some top professionals!—fail to focus on these critical issues?

I don't have an answer, but *you* are not going to fall into the same trap. Proper sound and lighting are not difficult once you begin to make them a priority.

Arrive at your venue early. Diligently plan, set up, and test, test, *test* the sound and lights. Get to know the tech folks. Make them your friends and allies. Always introduce yourself with a warm smile and handshake to anyone whose expertise—and key chain—could serve your needs.

When performing at a banquet, you also want to befriend the head waiter or maitre d'. That person can help with the overhead lights if there's no one else around, and can also ensure that tables are cleared and wait staff have exited the room before you make your entrance.

The performance area is where an entertainer earns his income (be it monetary or simply ego-gratification). When I am setting the stage for my performance and encounter a bit of resistance from some techie, emcee, or anyone else, I explain—always with a smile—that, "This is my office; this is where I work." It has to be perfect for me, comfortable and practical for the intended purpose. You may receive guileless assurances from techies that everything is just fine. Well, to use a phrase from the Cold War, "Trust, but verify."

I also explain that it's very much a win-win situation: when I look good, we all look good. Careful backstage preparation pays in offstage, after-the-show congratulations. *Don't back down.* Once you walk out there, it's *your* butt on the line, not theirs.

Later in this section, you'll read an anecdote about what can happen if you fail to follow the advice to take sound and lighting seriously.

Chapter 12

Sound

Sound Systems

The lack of appreciation for the importance of sound quality was exemplified by an online column I came across at a popular magic Web site. The author offered a fair amount of reasonable advice regarding the purchase of portable sound systems, but then he wrote a sentence that echoes the thinking of too many in our profession:

"Remember: you are only talking through the microphones so you won't require the dynamic range a singer or musician would."

And then later on in the same column...

"There are several more features of PA systems we can just summarily dismiss and save a few more bucks. First is the graphic EQ. Remember, you are simply amplifying your voice, not fine tuning it."

Wrong, wrong, wrong.

His last point assumes it is the quantity, not quality of your voice, that counts. He'd be correct if your job were calling out Bingo numbers. But the entertainer delivers more than raw information. He delivers his individuality, his emotions. With an adequate sound system, you hear a voice; with a *proper* sound system, you hear a personality. *You* are a personality.

Magicians and mentalists should place a high priority on finding, buying, and using a high-quality portable sound system. It's an *essential* investment, and you should purchase the best you can afford.

The author concluded his column with:

"Just remember, for 99.995% of you reading this, the most bare-bones PA system you can find will be best for you, so save that money for your next trip to the magic store!"

159

Follow his advice and that's where you'll be doing most of your performing: in the magic store.

But whether you bring your own or use a provided system, you must train your ears to differentiate between good and poor quality sound. Good sound means your voice has texture and warmth, and all words, in all registers, can be heard clearly.

Speakers

The audiovisual guys assigned to the hotel banquet hall where you'll be performing are often charming folks who sincerely want to help you look and sound your best. Don't be lulled into complacency by their friendly demeanor. And don't be intimidated if they come on with an I-know-what's-best-around-here attitude. They are not entertainers, they are geeks. Sweet, well-intentioned geeks, perhaps, but geeks nonetheless, and they don't know what you know.

Here's a scenario I have encountered frequently: if the A/V staff has access to four, six, or more portable speakers, they will gleefully place all of them around the room, including at the back of the room facing forward, so the sound shoots at the audience from all directions. That's bad. The speakers should help focus attention on *you*. Sound coming at the audience from everywhere seems to come from nowhere in particular.

Sometimes a room does require multiple speakers. More likely, however, a quality system consisting of just two speakers, properly set up prior to the show, can easily project your voice and music from the front stage area to the last row. And by using just two speakers, you achieve the effect you want: the sound projects forward from near where you are, and that helps ensure that you remain the center of attention.

Two top-of-the-line PA speakers from any of the leading manufacturers (Bose and JBL are among my personal favorites), coupled with a compatible and properly powerful amplifier system, can be configured to fill all but the largest auditoriums. I regularly took this approach in college auditoriums holding one thousand or more, with perfect sound quality and quantity. That is a better approach than placing more speakers around the room.

The A/V guys from the venue, or from the outside firm brought in just for the occasion, will fight you on this. They have the equipment, and they will want to use it. They might even goad you with "other performers love it." That's fine for other performers. They may not know what you (now) know, or need what you need. Or they may not care the way you now care about proper sound. Don't back down. You may need to finesse your way through, but keep in mind, when the show is over it's *you* they'll remember for better or worse, not the sound guy.

Testing, One... Two... Three

A simple test to see if the sound system works is not enough. Not nearly enough.

While it's best if the room is vacant during your sound check, that's not always feasible. During your setup, do not be shy about testing the sound system, even if people are milling around. Ignore them.

Here are the *essential* tips for testing:

- Speak softly into the microphone, then speak loudly. Any problems?
- Move around the stage to check for feedback and cable length problems.
- If you have enough cable, and certainly if you are using a wireless microphone, get off the stage and move around the room as much as possible, checking for feedback and dead spots.
- If you go into the audience during your show, you *must* go down among the seats during the sound check, and talk.
- Do you use music? Check every aspect of it: the cues to start and stop, the controls, the volume, the tonal quality (every venue responds differently to sound).

If you're not using a wireless microphone, have someone stand on stage and talk while you go to all parts of the room. If you do have a wireless microphone, take it out to where the audience will be and talk as you will be talking.

Listen.

Is your voice equally clear everywhere? If not, find out why, and see if it can be remedied. Sometimes a simple repositioning of the speakers is all that's needed.

During the show you will be talking at different volume levels; now's the time to learn if your soft phrases will be clearly heard, or if your loud exclamations will overload the system, so test your different voice levels.

Adjust the volume for maximum power and clarity. Adjust the tone; in general the human voice is best served by a mid-range setting between treble and bass. Don't fall into the trap that plagues so many DJs: they love bass for their music, and they pump it for their voices as well. The result is a muffled pea-soup-thick fog of sounds that were supposed to be words. We are among the performers who prefer to be understood.

The Beauty of the Handheld Microphone

Probably the most significant disagreement I have with other pros in my field is my advocacy for handheld microphones. Before we jump headfirst into this discussion, allow me a personal anecdote.

Over the years, I've received more compliments than I deserved, but two in particular stand out in my memory. The remarks were virtually identical, and twenty-four years separated them. Because they were uttered by fellow professional performers whom I respect, their words made me feel warm and fuzzy inside, and being that their observations were much more targeted than the usual "loved your show" comments all of us receive, the remarks reverberated and lasted longer in my memory.

The first was from Bob Cassidy, whose writings and lectures, to my mind, rank him among the top five innovators and analysts in the history of mentalism. The more recent one came from Jeff Evason, who, with his beautiful wife Tessa, presents the most thrillingly entertaining two-person mentalism act I've ever seen.

After seeing me perform, they both came over to discuss, in some detail, my "microphone technique." They both realized that for me, the microphone—the *handheld* microphone—did far more than amplify my voice. For me, it's a prop as important as any I've ever brought on stage. It should be for you as well.

A fixed-position microphone (clip-on or headset type) simply cannot offer the flexibility of a handheld! When a microphone is stationary, you have less control over the power and dynamics of your voice. It's a fixed distance from your mouth, and it remains at that distance throughout your show.

Our nearest relatives on the genealogy tree of performing artists must surely be the stand-up comics. Like us, they face their audiences alone, usually with material they've developed on their own. Yet unlike most of us, they almost always opt for a handheld microphone—at the comedy clubs, where they may not have much choice, and on the many TV specials that feature comics.

On his recent appearances on late night talk shows, America's reigning king of stand-up, Jerry Seinfeld, performed his routines and each time he used a handheld microphone. *Do you think it was because he doesn't know what to do with his hands?* No, he chose the handheld because of the control of his voice it affords him.

Yes, I know. You're a magician and you need to use your hands. I also know that in many cases it is perfectly feasible to rework parts of your act so that using a handheld is no longer a problem. I too need my hands during my act. But I blocked my routines so that:

- The microphone is on the mike stand for much of the act. At that point, both hands are free to point, gesture, display props, or do most anything, *or*
- I hold the microphone in one hand and do "stuff" with the other hand, *or*
- I could momentarily hold the microphone in my right hand with my forth and fifth fingers, leaving my thumb and two fingers free to work with my left hand, *or*
- I could, in a rare and *brief* moment, hold the microphone under my arm while I use both hands.

At all other times I simply hold the microphone and talk, unencumbered and in total control of my voice.

Sound like trouble? It's not. It merely takes some planning. Consider all the hefty advantages...

A handheld can give you a commanding presence; you talk loudly, but hold the microphone away from your mouth, creating an illusion that you have raised your volume more than you actually have.

Or you bring the microphone closer and talk softly. Suddenly you have created a sense of warmth, which again may be an illusion because the actual volume may not have changed all that much.

But best of all, a handheld allows you to whisper. You bring the microphone right up to your lips and whisper.

And do you know what happens when a performer whispers?

The audience perks up. They instantly know you are about to tell them something special. A breathy whisper, delivered slo-o-wly, with your lips right up against the microphone, can be a sledgehammer tool in the right hands at the right moment.

For example, try whispering the line...

"I really don't think this is going to work. Pray for me."

That line can be dramatic or funny, depending on who delivers it and the circumstances. The point is, when said oh-so-softly with the microphone held *up close to your lips*, it contrasts powerfully with your previous patter.

Yes, you can do all those techniques with a fixed-position microphone—talk loudly, talk softly, whisper—*but they won't have the same impact.* Not even close.

Then too, there's the problem of dealing with volunteers who join you on stage. Here's the typical scenario when the performer works with a clip-on microphone.

"And what was the word you selected out of thousands?"

"elhfkhdf"

"Elephant! Just as I had written on this board! Thank you very much!"

Volunteers talk to you on stage in a conversational voice. Why wouldn't they? They are talking to you and you are no farther away than anyone engaged in normal conversation. And they almost surely don't know how to project their unamplified voices.

If you use a clip-on, is there a way around this problem? Sure. You simply ask the volunteer to speak into your lapel. Yeah, that's classy.

On the other hand—literally—when I hold the microphone I control who gets heard and what gets heard. And as you know, you seek to Control Every Moment.

Then there's the particular benefit for magicians of the handheld microphone—the stage whisper. Momentarily drop the microphone to your side and your sotto voce instructions will not be heard. Again, that's a powerful tool not easily available to the clip-on addicts.

And now we come to one of the gilt-edged reasons for using a handheld: you can capture the Reaction. Recall the importance of Reactions, as spelled out in Section II. If you have a volunteer or two on stage, they become the eyes and ears of the audience, and we assume you brought them onstage to astound them. When the climax occurs, some people erupt in a clearly seen display of emotion. But others deal with astonishment internally, offering few visible clues about how you have scrambled their brains. For those moments, nothing beats having a handheld microphone, which you deftly move into place with perfect timing and which catches the softly uttered *"holy shit..."*

The audience long remembers those moments.

Respecting the Spectator

There is a huge gap in show-biz logic when I watch a performer who is wearing a clip-on mike talk to a volunteer on stage. If you are that performer, first acknowledge that your voice will be noticeably louder than the volunteer's voice. Now let's consider the possibilities. Are the spectator's responses not important? Or just not as important as what you, the star, has to say? If the responses are not important, *why did you ask the spectator anything?*

Yet I have seen this breach of judgment from performers at every level.

You can't have it both ways; the spectator's voice either is or is not important. Make a decision about this, and then choose your microphone.

Gear for Workers

To my mind, the best microphones for stage performers are the Shure "58" line, the ice-cream-cone-shaped mikes. Here are a few of their considerable features and benefits, as listed in a catalog:

- frequency response specially tailored for speech intelligibility
- steel mesh ball grille with integral 'pop' filter that minimizes wind and breath percussive sounds
- an on/off switch (in the PG58 model); (By keeping your thumb on that switch you gain even better control over stage whispers.)

Next best is the cylindrical Shure SM57. Both the SM57 and the microphones in the "58" line are appropriately and correctly described in catalogs as the "workhorses" of stages and studios, and as "true audio legends."

The microphone stand will usually have just one available clip to hold the mike, but that might not be the best one for your purposes. It is a good idea to carry different clips to accommodate different stands and different mikes, as well as differing connectors. (The "58" line microphones are superb at minimizing the sounds created when you put it on or remove it from the microphone stand.)

To summarize, I know I won't win many converts within the magic community, but I am convinced that the handheld microphone offers you superior and necessary control of your own voice and that of the spectators.

166

To Mike or Not to Mike?

A question for you: you've been hired to perform for an audience of fifty people in a room just large enough to seat them comfortably. Do you set up your sound system? Come on, answer that.

At New York City's wonderful Monday Night Magic, a typical audience consists of approximately 200 spectators (of which, I was told, usually no more than about five are magicians) and much of the time they do, in fact, have a full house. The staff rarely uses the sound system to amplify the voices of the performers, most of whom are full-time professionals.

Would you?

You should. It's a major miscalculation to work without a microphone in such situations. A couple of performers with whom I spoke at Monday Night Magic told me they didn't use the sound system because the room is small enough for their voices to be heard by every patron. And they're correct—they can be heard. But they miss the bigger issue. When you're on stage, you don't want to be equal to the spectators. You want to be figuratively larger than they are, more in control of every element than anyone else in the room. You cannot adequately control a laughing, responding, applauding audience without amplifying your voice. Period. If you think otherwise, you are fooling yourself.

The microphone allows you to goose a laugh into a bigger or more sustained laugh by tacking on a secondary booster joke just as the laugh begins subsiding. This is a technique I use in every one of my shows, and it would be impossible without a microphone. And the same applies to talking over applause; without a sound system, you must wait for the sounds from the audience to dissipate, and that once again means you are ceding control to something external.

Audiences are accustomed to hearing amplified voices. You adjust the volume, beforehand, so that you obtain just the vocal boost you need without overpowering anyone with sound waves.

Other than in a true close-up situation, you should always amplify your voice.

167

Monitors

You *must* hear what the audience hears. I never understand why so many performers overlook this simple requirement.

If you don't have audio monitors and the house speakers are placed in front of the stage, you will have a tendency to talk too loudly. (It's the same phenomenon we see with cell phone users who shout into their phones; they subconsciously expect the same earpiece volume they hear from their home phones.)

Insist on monitors. Without monitors, you will not hear what your audience hears; they hear sound emanating directly from the speakers while you hear your voice reflected back at you. That puts you at a substantial disadvantage.

An alternative to using monitors is to have two or more speakers that will serve as both the house public-address system and as your monitors. Position the speakers so they are as far back behind you as possible, then aim them diagonally across the room, so that the speaker over your right shoulder broadcasts out to the far left corner, and the opposite for the other speaker.

Caution: The audio guy will look at you like you are a pathetic show business neophyte who doesn't understand about feedback. Be patient with him. He's not an entertainer. The fact is, with most high-quality sound systems, you can stand almost directly in front of the speakers without causing feedback, especially if you're using a good handheld microphone. Condenser mikes, and especially clip-on condenser mikes, will give you more feedback problems (just one more advantage of the handhelds).

If you do have unacceptable feedback, you can try several possible remedies. First, if possible, change microphones; they each respond differently in different acoustic environments. Adjust the positions of the speakers; sometimes re-aiming them by just a few degrees will fix the problem. Also, try tweaking the tone controls; bringing one of the treble slides down a few notches might make all the difference.

But whatever you do, don't go on if you cannot hear what the audience hears.

Music

Frankly, if I were easing my way back into full-time performing, I would focus much of my energy on working more music into my act. Music by itself delivers an emotional kick, and when combined with your actions or words on stage almost always enhances the entertainment experience. Few acts cannot be embellished, if not significantly improved, by the judicious use of music. Certainly, David Copperfield and his team owe much of their success to their brilliant use of recorded music.

In the sport of figure skating, competitors and their coaches devote long hours to the careful selection of music to establish the perfect mood. All great movie directors depend on the Bernard Hermanns, John Williamses, and Elmer Bernsteins of the world to build plot points. In our field, little has been written about this important subject, but that may be a reflection of the fact that each individual performer must find his or her own best musical accompaniment.

Music can be used to:

• Cover slow moments, such as when volunteers come up to the stage and when they return to the audience
• Build tension
• Enhance frivolity
• Signal a climactic moment

Specific to our field, music can play a significant role in the magical process itself, by overriding other sounds. Stage whispers can be muffled out. You can ask a volunteer her name and later use that information for laughs or otherwise. The telltale noises emitted by certain effects can be concealed.

In the "Reactions" chapter, I wrote about targeting your words and actions. Music, too, must be similarly targeted toward a specific reaction. A particular piece might be:

• Funny
• Inspirational
• Dramatic
• Soothing
• Romantic

Before you pick out your music, decide where you're headed, and only then seek out the music that best gets you there.

There are several types of mistakes performers make when using music. First, there are the inappropriate choices. Two recent examples I've seen:

- Circus-theme music as volunteers walked up to the stage. This felt like a slight put-down of the volunteers.
- A mentalist uses the theme from the television show *Jeopardy* for his dramatic climax. The music produces a laugh, which is good, but it breaks the tension he is building, so for that specific time it is a poor choice.

Next is the problem of music clichés. One knowledgeable friend pointed out that during the last quarter of the 20th century it seemed half the magicians who used music used the same ten or twelve pieces. That's probably correct—and insane! The world is awash in royalty-free music. Go find something that doesn't make you sound like the guy on the Ed Sullivan show in 1965! And do we need another piece of magic performed to *Thus Spoke Zarathustra* (popularized in the film *2001, A Space Odyssey*)? I don't think so.

A final problem is the use of less than stellar audio equipment. Sound *quality*, in case you've missed the point of this chapter, is important! Spend the money necessary to give your audience a superior aural experience, not just an adequate one.

Of course, for most of magic's history, music required the services of live musicians. Then came vinyl records, various tape technologies, and the leap to compact disks. Yet controlling the music remained difficult and cumbersome, until the advent of the self-controlled systems that now utilize CDs, MP3, and MiniDiscs. Soon we will use whatever else is on the horizon. A vast panoply of possibilities is available to performers for whom music was never before a practical option.

Read the next section carefully. Then, if you don't already, give strong consideration to adding music to your act.

Control Yourself! You're in Public!

Unlike so many other areas of endeavor, the technology for performing magic and mentalism has changed little over the past few decades. Except for sound. Here, the big breakthrough is in the ability of the performer to control the sound, including the music. This truly smashes the old paradigm, in which the performer depended completely upon either live musicians or an "audio" person for the correct volume, the timing of effects, starting and stopping music, etc.

In the online *About.Magic* newsletter (magic.about.com) of March 5, 2003, the (now former) editor and guide, Bryan Dean, posted an article enumerating the virtues of one such device, the Virtual Soundman 7, and I've chosen, with permission, to reproduce part of it below (slightly edited). *This is not an endorsement*; I know that competitive systems will leapfrog each other in features and pricing. I include it here to highlight a few of the benefits these systems can offer. Undoubtedly, the manufacturers will continue to evolve and improve their products, and this information will be quickly outdated, yet it's important to emphasize the amazing capabilities out there now. (In the not-distant future we will look back at these systems as "quaint... and so expensive!")

Here's Bryan:

If you have ever been onstage and tried to control your own sound, you know how nightmarish that can be, right? Running offstage to hit the button and again to move it to the next track, etc. What a recipe for an unprofessional-looking show!

Well, the answer to that is the Virtual Soundman 7 (VS7) by Majiloon (majiloon.com). Kelly Duro is the electronic genius who put this device together. Unlike the more expensive ShoTech, the VS7 doesn't control things like a flashpot or lights; it controls the sound (and some special FX triggers, which are extra). And that's good, because if you don't need the bells-and-whistles, you won't be paying for features you don't (or won't) use!

I had the VS6 for the past year and loved it, but it needed a few features added. The VS7 is fantastic as (for me) it has all the features I need to control my sound:

Auto Remote Start-Up *— When ready, just press the "Play" button on the remote and it syncs the MiniDisc player with the VS7. So easy!*

Auto Pause *— If you ever need to pause your music and your hands are "full" (if you're juggling or doing card fans, for instance), you can program a pause right into the music.*

Auto Mute *— Some CD or MiniDisc players have a "beep" played when they play a track. The Auto Mute hides this beep automatically.*

Auto Cue Advance *— No more guessing... when you fade the music (or pause it) the VS7 will cue to the next track. (With the VS6, I could never remember if I'd advanced to the next track and I'd get all screwed up with the music order. Now, I don't have to think about it!)*

Anti-Sleep *— Some MiniDisc players tend to "sleep" when inactive. The VS7 will keep this from happening allowing you instant access to your music.*

Auto-Fade *— A great feature retained from the VS6: Just press two buttons simultaneously and the music fades, advances to the next track, then brings the sound up to the regular level and holds the track at "Pause".*

NiMh Rechargeable Battery *— A no-memory battery that charges in just a few hours. You can also power the VS7 with the included power adapter.*

A Built-In Speaker *— What a wonderful feature! Instead of pulling out your entire sound system to test your tracks, just use the built-in speaker.*

Optional LED Display Box *— This is great... a feature I needed and requested. The LED Box is a large display that shows the current track playing or on pause. Excellent, if you need to skip a track and need to know the next tune to be played will be the correct one.*

172

Optional Music Interrupt Circuit — *(I call it The 6th Button.) It's a feature I asked Kelly for and he put it in! You see he had an auto-ducking feature built in. This is where the sound would "duck" or fade out if the microphone was used. But, I told him that my Passport has that already and I would like to have control of the ducking since I had to actually run to the Passport to disengage it. The 6th Button will turn it on and off. Yay!*

Choice of AM or FM transmitter — *You'll need to visit the Majiloon site for the details about this, but I have the FM transmitter as I think it is more reliable. It's $50 more, but you get better distance.*

The basic price for the VS7 is $749.99; additional items like the LED box, FM transmitter, ankle switch, special effect triggers, etc., are extra.

Who wouldn't want all that?

As stated above, this is just one of the controllers out there. Other performers extol the virtues of Kerry Pollack's *ShoTech* system (wirelesswizardry.com). Do your due diligence, and then invest in the system that best meets your needs. I can't imagine you'll ever regret it.

Chapter 13

Lighting

He ["Dr. Phil" McGraw] puts in 18-hour days and talks to Oprah every night by phone. "Of course, she gives me pointers," he says. "She tells me, 'Take it from me, lighting is everything.'"

TV Guide, Sept 21, 2002

Who knew? America's billionaire Queen of Daytime TV owes her fortune to the placement of a few Klieg lights.

Well, lighting may not be *everything* for you, but lighting should never be treated lightly.

Here's what you do when setting up.

First, and absolutely most importantly, your stage needs what lighting designers call a good "wash" of light: general illumination for every area where any action takes place. (For this discussion, we will ignore any specific needs for darkness you might require to accomplish the magic.) And for most platform performers, a good wash is all they need. Umm, I'm talking lighting here.

In general, the more light the better. At an absolute minimum, you want to ensure that more light falls on you than on the audience. That should be obvious, but I have seen many professional speakers, and some entertainers, ignore this basic requirement.

Spotlights

Some venues pay extra for an operator to aim a follow-spotlight at the performers. Does that work for you? In my work as a hypnotist and mentalist, I need to work directly with the audience, and spotlights, depending on their position and intensity, can be blinding. So I ask the operator just to widen the aperture as much as possible, then center the beam and lock it into position. Usually that makes them happy (less work), and it makes me happy.

On the other hand, spotlights—and there may be more than one—do help focus attention on you, so you may choose to let the operators do what they're there for. Just be sure to get your butt up on the stage, and walk around in exactly the same lighting you will encounter during the show, spotlights following you and all. You can't know if the conditions suit you until you thoroughly test them. For most types of shows, you will want to raise the spotlights up as high as possible on their stands so the bright lights are not shining into your eyes as you try to make eye contact with the audience. Performers look foolish and amateurish when they need to shade their eyes to converse with someone in the audience. That should never happen if you properly set the lights beforehand.

Try to avoid performing with no light other than one strong spotlight. A powerful spotlight is harsh, casting stark and distracting shadows. You may be better served by turning on whatever lights are overhead, even fluorescents, if they help fill out the overall light pattern better. (Magic conventions are notorious for poor lighting, and for using spotlights inappropriately.) Unless you are certain you specifically want the dramatic effect it provides, don't settle for just one spotlight.

Finding the Hot Spot

If you're working without a spotlight, you face a different set of challenges. First, where will you plant yourself for most of your show? In most cases, lighting dictates the answer. You want to be smack in the brightest spot on the stage.

Here's how you find that spot without bothering anyone else. Stand where you think the most light falls. With luck (and usually), this will be downstage center, but not always. That's why you must test for what feels like the hot spot by moving slightly to your left, then to your right, forward and then back. Then proceed to the next part of the process.

Step to the side and just slightly in front of where you assume the hot spot is. Hold your hand up, palm facing the audience, where your head would be. Now move your hand slowly from side to side and front to back. Watch your palm. Does it get brighter or darker as it moves?

Once you find your hot spot, place the microphone stand on it and announce, *"Please do not touch this stand!"* (good luck) or, better, mark it on the floor with tape.

Re: Sound and Lighting.
Dominate the Terrain—An Object Lesson

The June 2003 Meeting of the Minds (as the Psychic Entertainers Association calls its annual get-together) in Calgary, Canada, was a festive, four-day event. On the final night, Saturday, PEA members from around the world dined, chatted, and applauded as awards were presented honoring the commitment of its members, some of whom had participated in the organization for its entire twenty-five years.

At the conclusion of the award ceremony, the membership prepared to be entertained by some of their own. Of the five acts that would be performing that night, three were full-time professionals, performers who earn their living by dependably delivering entertainment. The venue was a large ballroom in a fine Calgary restaurant, complete with sunken dance floor and terraced dining area. All signs pointed toward success. The crowd was fully primed, crammed with friends plus a good number of outsiders, drawn to the event by publicity, which included coverage on the local TV news shows.

But much of the night turned into a performer's (and an audience's) nightmare. From the very first act, the sound system seemed demon-possessed, shrouding each performer in a cocoon of squeals, hisses, shriekings, and gibberings. The sound system cut in and out, randomly but regularly, and effectively stymied the world-class performers who struggled heroically to adjust.

The next morning, Sunday, standing before the bleary-eyed PEA attendees, I began my annual Performance Workshop, a "director's" assessment of everyone's performances at the Meeting of the Minds' evening shows. When I reached the point where I was to review the Saturday night show, I stepped to the edge of the platform and brought the handheld microphone close to my mouth. I felt my voice thicken and experienced deep surprise at the sudden surge of emotion traveling up my spine. I described the debacle with the sound system the previous night and then said, "If I had been on the show last night, that never would have happened."

The lecture room fell silent. I repeated myself, more slowly, my voice a near-whisper in the charged silence of the lecture room.

*"If I had been on the show last night, that would **not** have happened."*

Does that sound pompous? Perhaps here, on this cold page, it does.

But my peers in the audience recognized that I was speaking from a place of sincerity, of camaraderie, of honesty, and I was banking on the professionalism and commitment to excellence within our organization to get a fair hearing. It was a matter of personal pride; the reputation of an organization I cared deeply about had been sullied. Here was a situation that, however unpleasant, needed to be addressed.

The Search for Remedies

In the case of the Saturday night performance at the Calgary Meeting of the Minds, although the bulk of the audience consisted of PEA members, at least a quarter of the attendees had paid to see us that night. *Civilians were present.* All shows matter, but when it's more than "just the guys" in the audience, they matter more. Your reputation rises or falls every time you step in front of an audience.

Can you imagine the word-of-mouth generated by that Saturday night performance? Remember, as far as the audience is concerned, *there are no excuses.* They arrive at a venue, pay good money, and expect to be entertained. They will make no fine distinctions: "Oh, the performer did his best under very trying circumstances. How could the venue treat that nice performer that way?" From the perspective of the general paying audience, you *are* the venue. And they will no more overlook the shortcomings of your performance than they would accept the apologies of a restaurant waiter who offers: "I'm sorry the salad greens are wilted. But it is not our fault. The cooling system in the produce truck failed. All we had left were these. However, I made sure to polish your silverware with extra care."

How generously would you tip that waiter? Would you return?

Where the Buck Stops

The only way that you can hope to overcome the kinds of problems experienced at the Calgary MOTM is to own the territory. *Dominate the terrain.* The performer who wants to succeed in every circumstance needs to take *every* performing situation and venue seriously and become as affably stubborn, finicky, and particular as you are about the things in your life that you depend upon for comfort and safety. Would you drive around in your car without a spare tire? Continue to operate a computer holding your list of performing dates for the coming months without backing it up?

You must take control. And responsibility. Otherwise, you will find yourself looking out across the footlights with that deer-in-the-headlights expression on your face as the Sound System from Hell chews your carefully constructed performance into a thing of misery.

Blessed Are the Not-Meek

It amazes me how performers who seduce, charm, dominate, and fry audiences on a regular basis can be completely docile, tame, and undemanding in the presence of sound and lighting technicians on whom their shows—and the happiness of their audiences—depend. Statements that these powerful performers would not accept from other technical professionals, such as automotive repairmen ("Oh, that rattle is the way this year's model is supposed to sound!") seem to fly completely under the radar when uttered by the average sound and light technician. Every performer needs to take responsibility for an event. Take ownership.

While it is understandable that sound or light technicians will try to minimize their workload, skimping on the fine details by telling you that "everything was up and working fine last night," you do not have the luxury to go with their untested assertion. As a professional performer, you have a duty to go through the checklist and perform the necessary tests to ensure your own success.

Your absolute lifeline as a performer, the only thing that connects you to your audience, unless you happen to perform as a mime—without music—is the sound system. Losing that lifeline, or worse, having it turn into a spitting monster spraying your audience with vile sonic effluvia as it did to the performers in Calgary, is professional suicide.

When I asked one of the performers if he had done a sound check before the performance, I was told, "Sort of." We need look no further for the roots of the problems in Calgary that night. Sound checks are not an optional part of a performer's life. Like good dental hygiene, sound fiscal habits, and backing up your hard drive, men and women who ignore these routine but important parts of life will—in most cases—reap the eventual consequences of their neglect.

This was certainly true that night in Calgary.

What would I have done before the Calgary performance? Since I was not backstage before the show I cannot provide absolute answers. But, based on what I was told later on, I do know this:

A number of microphone options were available. At the moment I realized there were serious audio problems, I would have sought out the simplest, most direct solution: a corded handheld microphone and a microphone stand. This setup is direct and simple. If you can solve a room's problems with this setup, you go with it, even if you regularly use a cordless, clip-on microphone. (Bad sound *ruins* a show, so you accept a work-around solution. A few awkward moments are better than constant craving for aural relief.)

The room had large, disco-type speakers around its ceiling and sides and, in the rear, a DJ booth with the sound system controls. I would have tested:

- various mikes, and for each I would have adjusted the tone, volume, and other controls to find its optimum quality
- turning different speakers on and off
- re-aiming speakers
- combinations of all the above.

And I would have taken these steps until I was certain I had achieved the best solution available.

Get it right, whatever the cost in time. An audience will barely remember a delay if it's followed by a successful performance. But they'll forever associate your name with the unpleasantness of having their ears horribly violated by the Devil's Own Sound System.

Count on that—and act accordingly.

Chapter 14
Before the Show

Know Your Audience

You need to ascertain, if only in the broadest terms, who will be facing you. You may pull out the same tricks for the Boy Scouts or a senior citizens group, but at the very least, your pacing will be different.

Beyond the age range, you want to know the type of person out there. Business audiences are not all the same; salespeople do not respond the same as senior management.

When performing for religious organizations, check to see if there are sections of your act that might offend or seem out of place. The mentalist especially needs to tread lightly here; some groups contend that looking into the future or unraveling hidden thoughts is expressly prohibited, and they will recite scripture to prove their point. Don't argue with them. You're not likely to change anyone's mind, regardless of how carefully you frame your rebuttal.

Then there's the performer's nightmare, which, if you stay in this business long enough, will happen to you while your eyes are open and you're fully awake: the audience that doesn't speak your language. You assume that the folks who brought you in for the occasion would never let this befall any performer, but it has happened to me and many of my performing friends. That's why you want to ask just a few basic questions ahead of time.

Then there was the time I was booked to do my hypnosis show, and only after I stepped on stage did I learn that a large percentage of my audience was hearing-impaired. When I turned to the woman who booked me to ask about the situation, she said, "Don't worry, they read lips." Wonderful, I thought to myself; one of the first things I say to my onstage volunteers is, "When I count to three, close your eyes..."

Forewarned is forearmed. Ask these questions well before you step onto the stage.

Setting the Environment

Arrive early, while the room is being set up. This is your opportunity to turn the venue into *your* space, your office, your place of business. Don't blow it.

Get to know whatever staff may be assigned to the room for your event: audiovisual technicians, the maitre d', the head porter who's setting up the tables and chairs, the backstage crew, etc. Politely introduce yourself, smile, and say their name back to them as you shake hands. Much of the time they go about their jobs unrecognized, especially by "talent," and the simple act of acknowledging their worth will help create an ally. In show business, you need all the friends you can muster.

Survey the general situation:

- Are there doors near the performing area that might open during your set?

- If people need to take a bathroom break while you're on, what will be their path? For both of the above scenarios, try to position your performance area so you will be subjected to the fewest distractions possible. You may even be able to deputize one or two people to act as ushers.

- Do you know where the room's lighting controls are? Many times lights have gone dark while I was performing, because someone unknowingly leaned against a switch. If you know the location of those switches, you can immediately resolve the problem. Even when you have people from the hotel or organization doing the sound and/or lights for you, they sometimes aren't around when things go wrong. The more you know about the situation, the better.

At the risk of being overly dramatic, think of your performance as a battle for which you need allies to overcome obstacles. Every venue presents a new set of obstacles that must be discovered, and then tamed.

An audience begins as a group of individuals; as your act progresses, it coalesces into a sentient collective being that responds to the stimuli you present.

You need to ensure that the audience members feel each other's emotions, and there is much you can do to help that process before you walk on stage.

Chairs

What do chairs in the audience have to do with maximum entertainment? Much more than most performers seem to realize.

When setting the room, remember two important things about chairs:

- The closer together, the better. You want people to hear the reaction of others—the laughs, the gasps, the applause. Do what you can to bring people together. Often the center aisle is wider than necessary. Reduce that by putting (or have someone place) one or two more chairs into the gap at the end of each row.

- Generally, the closer to you, the better. Often the front row is much farther back from the stage than it needs to be. You don't want to perform for a dead space; you want live onlookers. Again, fill that space by arranging for a row or two to be added.

Stay in this business long enough and eventually you'll be stuck presenting to a small crowd in a large room. That's a difficult situation and you want to avoid it, so before your show, try to get a last-minute approximation of the number of people expected and have the room set accordingly. If it becomes clear that too many chairs are set up, act immediately. First, remove excess chairs from the back of the room. People often have a phobia about sitting up front, and if you give them the opportunity to wander in and sit anywhere, they'll stay in the back, so get rid of those back rows. If the chairs are immovable, as in a theater, rope off the back sections. If you don't have people who can do these things at your direction, *you* do it!

Whenever possible, deputize assistants to actually escort audience members to their seats, with instructions to fill in the front rows first.

If you walk out on stage and find a small audience scattered around a large room, within the first few minutes of your show politely, but firmly, tell the people in the back to move forward. "You'll enjoy the show much more from the front. Trust me; I've seen it!"

A related, high-octane tip: if you have people you need to impress—agents, meeting planners, girlfriend(s)—*be sure to seat them near the front.* This applies to virtually any live performance. Those up front experience a different show, a better show (sad to say), than those in the back.

You can easily prove that to yourself at any large-venue rock concert. Despite the fact that everyone is there because they very much want to be, you will *always* see less gyrating enthusiasm in the back sections than in the front.

There's a reason the cheap seats are cheaper.

Stairs or steps

If you use people from the audience on stage, ensure that there is an easy route for them to reach the stage. Ideally, two sets of stairs should lead from the audience to the stage. Walk on them yourself. Are they sturdy? If not, take action to fix the problem. If the steps do not have handrails, and your volunteers are women in heels, or anyone who seems the slightest bit unsteady because of age or having enjoyed the open bar, walk to the top of the stairs and offer your hand for assistance.

If the area immediately off the stage is dark, you might suggest that bright or luminous tape be placed on the top edge of each step.

Makeup

I'm not an expert on makeup, but in a moment you'll read the advice of someone who does fit that description. My major input comes down to this: too much is worse than none at all. If I'm sitting in the fifth row of a theater and I'm aware, as I was recently, of the rouge on the cheek of a male magician (*not* a clown!), it's a distraction.

Makeup should always be used when you have your publicity photos taken and when you do TV appearances. For my regular platform work, I rarely use makeup, other than the stick makeup specifically formulated for dark shadows under the eyes (or as I call them, excess baggage). I know several leading pros who have a similarly minimalist approach to "cover-ups." But in general, you do want to wear some makeup when working under bright full stage lights. For some, just a little powder to cut down the reflection may be sufficient. Or, for a simple, brainless standby used by many in the television industry (we used it in my Brooklyn College TV days and it's still used by many newsmen just prior to stepping before the cameras), turn to Max Factor Tan #2, lightly applied with a damp sponge. It obviously depends on your complexion, but that product suits most Caucasian men. And it's a good beard cover for five o'clock shadow.

Now to the expert. Paul Alberstat is a successful full-time performer with a couple of college degrees, including a BFA in theatre arts. I've read some of his writings about makeup, and it's clear that this man knows his stuff. Here's his mini-course on makeup for magicians and mentalists:

The best makeup to use is Ben Nye Creme stick. Go to a quality supplier, find a good match for your skin tone for the base, a good neutral powder (a large container... you can never have too much powder), a light blush and "lake" lip color (again, this is neutral for a man). Both a brown or black eye liner pencil (depending on your eye color), and a white eye liner pencil as well (which you use if you happen to have bloodshot eyes: lining the lower part of your lid helps to magnify the white and remove the red... a little tip if you are working on television or close-up situations without any other makeup).

The reason I prefer Ben Nye Creme is that when you powder after each step, you can literally erase any mistakes and continue, as opposed to having to remove everything and starting over. This is a big advantage. If it is a quality shop you are purchasing from, they should have a specialist who can show you how to apply everything, instructionally, which again is worth your while.

Always apply your makeup under incandescent lights, not fluorescent lights. The only time you apply makeup under fluorescent lights is when you are applying makeup for television, and truthfully, any good show will have a specific makeup artist there to apply it for you. The light and shadows are different when working on stage, and you need incandescent lighting to do your application correctly.

Get a pump bottle of fragrance-free hairspray (avoid lacquer sprays). This is used as a sealer before you apply any makeup at all. Just spray a light covering all over your face and wait thirty seconds for it to dry. This prevents any oils from coming up to the surface and blotching your makeup. This is a little secret that few know about. Those with particularly oily skin might apply witch hazel, or any similar astringent, prior to the spray. However, if you wash your face thoroughly right before you apply the makeup, you probably won't need the spray (or a more expensive oil-blocking "barrier" cream). The spray or crème is a good thing if you don't have the facilities for washing, or if you are in a hurry (the spray dries a lot quicker). If you apply powder after each step, the make-up should be fine without either one.

Don't forget the cold cream (like Nivea) and a good astringent like Bonne Bell "Ten-O-Six", as they will help immensely to remove the makeup later. You will also need some applicator sponges and brushes, plus some Q-tips and cotton balls.

Makeup, including street makeup, is supposed to improve your looks, not make you look as if you are painted! As you apply the base for your first few times, you should have someone a good distance away from the stage judge the application for you while you stand under those bright lights.

Finally, the best thing to do is to talk to a makeup specialist, not a woman behind a cosmetics counter. Go to a theatrical supply house that has a makeup specialist, or seek out a theatrical makeup artist and pay for a consultation. Have him or her match you with the best skin tone for you, along with the proper eyeliner color, blush, brushes, etc. In effect, you are having them put together a personalized makeup kit. Keep a list of everything in a separate place, so that you will always know what it is that you may need to replace in case something goes missing.

Thanks, Paul.

Malodorous Maladies, etc.

I hate to bring up these embarrassing subjects, but the older you grow, the more you realize that anyone can broadcast bad odors without being aware of it.

You ought to shower as close to show time as is practical, and always use a quality deodorant. (Some cheap ones smell foul!) Avoid heavy doses of aftershave lotion or cologne—what you find attractive may be repulsive to others.

Before your show, always execute a preemptive strike against possible offending breath; you don't want the folks on stage to back away from you. If possible, brush your teeth, and follow with mouthwash, or, at least, chew on a breath mint or two. In a pinch, grab some parsley garnish from the kitchen. It's a potent bad breath neutralizer.

Check yourself in a mirror. Up close! Without being overly graphic, check those orifices from which nasties might be protruding. Smile wide and check your teeth. Any spinach there? Then step back and check your total look. Are all your pocket flaps down? Is your tie straight? Is your jacket collar smooth?

Your Introduction

Don't take your introduction lightly. The way you're introduced directly and immediately affects the audience's expectations. In many cases, they have little or no idea who you are or what you do, and your intro becomes the welcome mat, their first step into your world.

Even when they do know about you, the intro sets the tone for the first few moments. Make it inviting, with just enough information to set the mood without becoming overly self-serving.

Now and then, someone will have already written your introduction. Your response must be along the lines of, "Great! Let me take a look at it just to make sure everything is correct." Chances are it won't be great, and you'll be glad you saw it beforehand.

Your introduction should:

- Be pre-written by you, with just a hint of what you're about to do.
- Include your best credits. This is your opportunity to have someone else brag about you... where you've performed, for whom, along with any honors, degrees, or other accomplishments that might be appropriate. Don't be shy! People like to know they are being entertained by a "star," even if they've never heard of you.
- BE TYPED IN ALL CAPS.
- Be rehearsed with the person who will be delivering it (a possibly awkward request, so if they hesitate, back off).

If you work with an assistant, it's insulting to the assistant if only your name is announced. This is especially true if the two of you appear together at the start. If she (it's usually a "she") is not present at the opening, then a one-name intro is acceptable, but she should then be acknowledged shortly after her appearance.

You need to discourage the emcee—firmly—from veering from your words. Ad-libs at this point rarely pay off.

The last thing the emcee will say is your name. Audiences have been preconditioned to begin clapping when they hear the name of the performer, so never place any words in your intro following your name.

"Please put your hands together..." is old school. The audience knows how to clap. Alternatives are:

- Please welcome, the amazing...
- Join me in welcoming to our stage...
- It's my pleasure to introduce... Mr. Joe *Blowhard!*

I always tell the emcee, with a smile, "The most important thing the emcee has to do is... make sure the performer is ready!" I say this lightheartedly, but I look right at them so they get the message that *I'm not kidding.* Twice in my early career I was introduced when I was nowhere in the vicinity; the audience started to dislike me before I set foot on the stage!

If you are using a microphone that is on the stage, the emcee must use that same mike for the introduction. If it's not working, that becomes his problem, not yours. Also, sometimes at a banquet, the emcee will want to introduce you from the dais. Awful idea! That would mean the audience looks at him and they must turn to face wherever you happen to be, and that leads to an awkward delay in getting your momentum.

A good part of the emcee's job is to get everyone's attention. Make it clear to him or her: "Do not introduce me until you have everyone in their seats and paying attention to *you.*" If, as I said, the microphone becomes unplugged, or a squeal of unexpected feedback sends hands to ears, or the stage lights aren't on—those problems must be discovered while the emcee is on stage, not after the star (*you*) has been introduced.

When you walk out, show the emcee respect by shaking his hand and thanking him, by name, and then acknowledge the audience. You might tell the emcee beforehand that you are going to shake his hand. If, however, the emcee walks off in the opposite direction, you either ignore him and acknowledge the audience, or you might, as I do, just play it for a laugh by extending your hand in his direction.

Just Before You Walk Out

Some performers drag themselves onto the stage looking defeated. Don't let that happen to you. Walk out with confidence!

If you have a tendency to slouch—and the older you get the more pronounced that tendency becomes—use this trick to get yourself ramrod-straight. Stand with your back against a wall or door. Straighten up so the backs of your shoes, the backs of your calves, your buttocks, your shoulder blades and the back of your head all touch the wall. Stay that way for five to ten seconds. Get the feeling of everything coming into alignment, then step away, maintaining that posture.

As the show progresses, gravity will pull you down, so make an effort to mentally snap back to the feeling you had when you stood against the wall. Slouched shoulders and drooping head signal age and world-weariness; a straight-arrow posture signals youthful vitality and self-assurance. As an entertainer, that's the image you want to project.

If your muscles feel tight while waiting to go on, stretch. (Actually, stretching is a valuable pre-show habit even if you don't think you are tight. It loosens the muscles and calms the nerves.) To stretch your neck muscles, which tend to tighten especially in the presence of excess nervous energy, roll your head around. This is not the time to feel self-conscious! If people do see you, they will assume this is what pros do before they step onstage.

Take a couple of deep breaths. You may be breathing shallowly without being aware of it, and that won't help you.

Have a large glass of water available backstage before you walk out, and another somewhere on the stage. Take a final sip.

A Personal Entertainment Highlight: David Copperfield — Flying

I can recall only two times when I literally experienced a visceral reaction to magic, when what I watched affected my gut. The two could not have been more different.

One was the Masked Magician. The smarmy mean-spiritedness of those shows appalled me as I watched them viciously attack a centuries-old tradition that lived inside me. I found myself crying out "Not the Linking Rings! Why? Why!?" and my stomach churned.

The exact opposite end of the physical-reaction spectrum happened during one of David Copperfield's TV specials. I saw Flying. It thrilled me to my core in a way no other trick has, before or since.

The perfect magic trick is the one you would do if you were truly a wizard. Vernon's Unlimited Production of Silver, done at the dinner table, or reaching into the air to produce coins, à la Miser's Dream, both meet that criterion. My favorite close-up effect (which apparently evolved from a Patrick Page concept) has many variations and names; it involves cleanly showing a stack of one-dollar bills and then changing them into higher denomination bills. Nothing but the bills and bare hands; when done by a professional (close-up pro Alan Scher is the best I've seen at this), it's remembered for years. And why not? It is exactly what you would do if you truly possessed magical powers.

What powers would a genuine Magician exhibit if he were to perform before a large audience? One answer lies both in mythology and superhero comic books. Man wants to leave Earth's grasp, to fly, to soar, not in a mechanical contraption, but the way a bird does. A bird thinks, in his little bird brain, "I'm here, and now I want to be there." If he's on the ground and wants to perch on a tree limb, he lifts his beak and up he goes. To earthbound man, that's magic of the highest order.

193

David Copperfield and his team have developed some of the slickest, most incredible illusions imaginable, and David performs them with icy-hot precision.

Then there's *Flying.*

In this perfectly executed routine, he shows us the purest of pure Magic. No props or assistants. No tables, swords, cloth coverings, water fountains, and certainly no brooms! The man looks up... and up he goes. Smoothly, he glides and swoops. And only after he has established his mastery of the air does he challenge the intellect by introducing hoops and transparent boxes, which affect his airborne antics not in the slightest.

Stylishly, thrillingly, and miraculously, David Copperfield *flew*, and inside my body, I felt as though *I* were soaring.

Watching *Flying* on Copperfield's *Illusion* DVD didn't diminish my admiration of this "trick" (what a trifling word in this case). Instead, seeing it with the sharpest video details and highest quality audio made it ascend still higher in my view.

Section VI

◀ PERFORMANCE ▶

"A presentation, especially a theatrical one,
before an audience."

Chapter 15
Close-Up Magic

The most-performed category of magic is the close-up kind. No scientific survey validates that observation, but one need merely peruse the magic magazines and catalogs to reach this conclusion. (By itself, card magic, which is almost always performed in an intimate setting, occupies a huge slice of the "magic-by-type" pie chart.) So while the guiding principles and strategies covered in this book apply to vast segments of the mystery-worker population, it makes sense to touch on some of the special situations and obstacles faced by the armies of close-up workers scattered across the globe.

Traditionally, the close-up worker deals with one of two scenarios. The first is the more difficult: you walk up cold to a group of people. They may be seated at a table, or they might be standing. In either case, you start as the outsider.

The easier situation is the warm start: they invite you over to their table, or they come to where you are, as in the Magic Castle.

In the first case, the cold start, your opening words take on even greater importance than normal. Frequently you will be interrupting a conversation, or worse, a meal, so it becomes critical that you ingratiate yourself quickly. Body language and attitude count more than canned words at this point. Some of the best close-up performers don't do or say anything related to magic when they first approach a potential audience, they simply chat for a while and use that interlude to assess the ambience and personalities of the group. Experienced workers are flexible enough to read the vibes and adjust the repertoire accordingly.

Pleased to Meet You?

Close-up workers often perform a continuing series of short sets, and that very fact can lead to performance fatigue. You must be aware of that tendency, and fight it. I hate seeing, as I have too many times, a performer who in any way conveys a feeling that he's done his seven-minute set fifteen times in the past two hours, and now he appears bored or distracted.

Don't let that be you. Get your energy level up, every time, before you approach a new group. Every group may include someone important, and every group may include a fuddy-duddy who will complain to the higher-ups if he is less than pleased with you.

So smile! Establish your human identity. Start that process by introducing yourself: "Hi, my name is Bob and I'm the magician here tonight. Do you have a minute for something *amazing*?"

Connect with me and the people I'm with. If you know you interrupted us, smile and *apologize* for the interruption (this appears to be an exception to my "never apologize" rule, but at this point, those folks are not yet your audience) and then immediately go into a strong, quick opener.

Do *not* say, "Would you like to see a trick?" Anyone can do a trick. You do miraculous things.

"You Want Me to Pick Another Card?"

One mistake close-up workers make too often is that they don't vary their effects enough. You *can* be wonderfully entertaining doing a parade of card tricks, as long as the plots don't overlap. Each new effect, card or otherwise, must showcase some new talent, skill, or "power," or develop a plot.

- First I'll find your hopelessly lost card.
- Then I will make it magically jump to another location.
- Now I can play poker with you and, despite your choosing who gets which cards, I still manage to win every time (perhaps softening the "loser" message with Harry Lorayne's clever running gag, "I *want* you to win").

The key here is that, aside from the method, each trick must *feel* as though you're showing them something quite different, even if it really is not. I've seen magicians do entertaining ten- or fifteen-minute sets that were based on little more than the repeated use of a well-executed double lift, yet each effect took the spectators into new emotional territory.

Surprise me, then surprise me again in the *way* you surprise me.

May I Borrow Your Wife...
I Mean, Your Watch?

One advantage the close-up worker has over the stage performer is the ability to borrow items from onlookers quickly and easily. Magic with *my* watch, *my* pen, or *my* ring will always have a head start over conjuring with your watch, your pen, or your ring.

Borrow objects when you need to, as long as it does not slow down the pacing or become a burden on anyone. If you need to borrow something that is not immediately at hand, do something—talk, juggle, or perform a quick trick—while the object is being retrieved. Never just stand around while the woman fumbles though her purse looking for the dollar bill you requested. Dead time sucks the life out of entertainment, so ensure that you do something that keeps the focus on you, not on the hunt for the greenback.

By the way, *please* don't neglect to return borrowed items! Think that's ridiculous advice? Not long ago I brought a neighbor to a New York City magic show. The magician borrowed my friend's $10 bill and did the usual "sucker" bits of business. Suddenly, he was taking his bows and exiting the stage! My friend looked at me... "Isn't he supposed to give me the money back?" Later, while we happened to be dawdling on the street outside the theater, deciding where to grab a bite to eat, the magician turned up with the bill and said, "I knew I'd find you out here." Yeah, right.

My guess is that we weren't the only ones in the audience who noted this lapse, but we probably were the only ones who knew the debt actually was repaid. Not a great impression to leave on an audience!

May I Borrow Your Hand...
The Clean One?

In general, the strongest tricks are those that happen in the hands of the spectators. (In my early days when I was doing mentalism on cruise ships, I incongruously included an interlude with sponge balls! A woman shrieking in surprised delight is a reaction that's hard to top, so—despite conjuring dogma against mixing magic and mentalism—it stayed in my program for several years.) Magic books and catalogs are jammed with in-the-hand tricks, and the wise close-up magician develops one or two such killer routines.

A few basic guidelines must be observed when touching spectators:

- Be sure your hands are clean, and that no one has seen you blowing your nose or doing anything else off-putting.

- Be sure the objects you place in the hands appear reasonably sterile.

- Treat the spectator with respect. I have seen magicians manhandle hands and arms when placing sponge balls ("Hold them *tight! Tighter! Higher!*) or other objects into the spectator's grasp.

- Give extra attention to your verbal instructions. If it is imperative that the hand not be opened prematurely, look right into her eyes and say, "Don't open your hand until...!" If she does blow the ending, understand it was *your* fault, not hers.

Finally, on the subject of magic with borrowed objects, a mini Personal Entertainment Highlight goes to Gregory Wilson's *On The Spot* video. Every routine on this two-tape set is performed out in the real word, and with only a few minor exceptions, everything is truly impromptu; no cards, just items real people have about them. All the routines are good, and some are great, but I mostly love this video because of the reactions Gregory gets from the spectators. I laughed when he did his version of Slydini's Paper Balls Over the Head for a couple of young women at an outdoor bar, then I laughed during the "explanation" in the studio (using an eye-candy model/actress) and then I laughed the most when, to close tape number one, he was back out at a different bar and did it again for another young woman and her friends. Her gentle but increasing frustration at objects mysteriously disappearing from view simply becomes funnier and funnier. Gregory's magical "moves" on this tape show us nothing ground-breaking, but his people-management skills, and the joy he elicits from his spectators, serve as admirable targets for our own entertainment aspirations.

"And All I Gotta Do Is... Act Naturally"

The performer who works in intimate settings must, more than others, avoid pretense, unnecessarily loud speech, and overly dramatic gestures. The best close-up workers I've seen blend into the ambience and rhythms of the room. You can be hilarious without resorting to clownish behavior, and by appearing to be a normal human being your tricks seem even more amazing.

Listen to what they say to you and react to it, just as you would in any typical social situation. If you act like a robot, you'll be treated like one. People respond to each other, and you should never break that line of normal human interaction.

Never stop a spectator from talking, especially if you're the one who's moved into their space. They want to be a part of the fun, and you have no moral authority to stop them, certainly not at first, and usually never during your time with them.

Take control, but be aware that the more intimate the setting, the more subtle and understated you must be. Not everyone understands the dynamics of the show-biz situation the way you do, and this is especially true for close-up and walk-around performers. What right do we performers have, to expect anyone to adhere to our concepts of proper decorum, especially if we have thrust ourselves into a group? We have no such right, so we must bend to fit the dynamics of the group we're joining, invited or otherwise. After a while (and if you're good it could be after just a minute or two), you can begin to exert control.

Never intimidate. At all costs, avoid words, facial expressions, and gestures that in any way suggest displeasure. These lead to tension, and tension subverts entertainment. Always remain polite and friendly.

Chapter 16
Mentalism

I love tennis, and have spent a ridiculous fortune on lessons. But to the glee of my opponents, I stink at it. I blame this distressing lack of skill on the fact that I took up the game in my forties. My bad habits were unbreakable, so I never developed the strokes my son mastered by the time he was ten.

A similar phenomenon exists when a performer branches from magic into mentalism. It seems the more years a person steeps himself exclusively in magic, the more difficult it becomes to understand the dynamics of successful and entertaining mentalism.

Mentalists are well aware that, within the magic community at large, many believe the phrase "entertaining mentalism" to be an oxymoron. (And some of my PEA buddies would be pleased if I allowed magicians to continue believing that.) Magicians who deride mentalism tend to know the art only from seeing it performed in magic settings, and I am the first to agree that in those settings it usually *is* boring and difficult to watch.

That's not the mentalism I care about and love. If you haven't seen the modern masters of the field—Gil Eagles, Marc Salem, Tim Conover, Ross Johnson, the Evasons, Gerry McCambridge, Kreskin, Derren Brown, to name just a few of *many*—you have no idea how powerfully mentalism can affect and entertain an audience.

To illustrate the limited understanding of mentalism strategies among magicians, here's a quote from Darwin Ortiz's incredibly comprehensive and overwhelmingly right-on-target book, *Strong Magic; Creative Showmanship for the Close-Up Magician*:

A very subtle use of the accidental convincer is provided by Juan Tamariz in a book test taught in his The Five Points in Magic. *He wishes to force the seventh word on page 106. Having forced the page, he tells the spectator to add the digits of the page number to arrive at one word on the page. Since one, zero, and six add up to eight, he tells her, she should look at the eighth word.*

Naturally, someone in the audience is bound to point out that one, zero, and six add up to seven, not eight. The performer responds by saying, "Of course, you are right... excuse me! It does not matter: the seventh word." Through a cleverly staged accident, the performer has convinced the audience that he could just as easily divined the eighth word or, by implication, any other word in the book.

Here we have two major figures, Ortiz and Tamariz, each a highly respected performer and philosophizer in the magic world, writing about mentalism and veering wildly off course. This is mentalism as presented at magic conventions. None of the mentalists cited above would *ever* perform this routine—at least not as written.

What's wrong?

Mentalism, at its most effective, should be presented as if the performer truly could do what he claims (and I will tell you, not everything working mentalists do is a "trick" in the magician's sense of the word). So, in demonstrating what we would call a book test, a *real* mindreader would ask you to open a book to any page, think of one of the words you see there, close the book, and he would then reveal the word. The further one deviates from that ideal, the less convincing it becomes.

In mentalism, "convincing" correlates strongly with "entertaining." If the audience just assumes it's all a magic trick (I deal with the subject of disclaimers later) the entertainment value plummets. That, in large part, is why mentalism causes eyes to glaze over when performed at magic get-togethers: magicians refuse, or are genetically unable, to suspend their disbelief. Plus, magicians want clever moves and gimmicks, and mentalism usually has neither.

The Tamariz routine, in just those two brief paragraphs, fails for several specific reasons:

- No real mind reader would ask that digits be added together. If you don't immediately accept this concept, skip this chapter.

- A mentalist, by implied definition, is a person with superior mental abilities. Would he have trouble adding one, zero, and six? And since the routine, as presented, suggests that he stumble over the simple addition, he looks momentarily foolish. Who would want that?

(Although it may work for Tamariz, thanks to his hyperkinetic stage persona.)

- *"Naturally, someone in the audience is bound to point out that one, zero, and six add up to seven, not eight."* This assumes that:

  a) the audience is paying close attention,

  b) some brave soul will risk embarrassing the star of the show by pointing out how foolish (see second bullet, above) he is, and

  c) said brave soul is certain he himself won't be embarrassed.

All in all, it's too big an assumption.

- The page has been forced; the routine has already moved away from the ideal book test. Now another level of complexity is tacked on to arrive at the word.

- The spectator is asked to count to the eighth, or seventh, word. What's happening while that counting is going on? Usually, nothing, because the performer can't risk distracting the spectator and causing a miscount.

- Regardless of the situation, in some cases the spectator *will* miscount and end up on the wrong word. A working mentalist, or anyone else hoping to present entertaining mentalism, cannot take that chance.

One or two of the above "problems" may be acceptable, but in this case we just have too many. All magic gains in entertainment value when the plot is direct and unencumbered with detours, and this dictum is particularly true in mentalism. This Tamariz routine will mystify many viewers, but it also imparts a psychological residue that "something's amiss here."

Strong, entertaining mentalism is clean mentalism: "Think of something; I'll tell you what it is."

Ironically, directly after the two paragraphs on the Tamariz routine, Ortiz writes about another pre-planned "accidental convincer" used by the late German mentalist Punx. Until his health failed, Punx was a member of the PEA, and performed for us on a couple of occasions. He was a true mentalist. The convincer he used, as cited by Ortiz, was of a different magnitude. Punx would sometimes unfold a billet and turn it 180 degrees before reading it. In fact, the billet was blank, and Punx was "actually reciting from memory the spectator's writing which he previously glimpsed," the implication being that the writing was upside down when he first unfolded the paper. That move, the turn of the paper, aligns perfectly with the actions we might see if the routine was performed by a person—psychic or otherwise—who simply happened to open the paper and saw that the writing was upside down.

Disclaimers

Few topics are as hotly debated within and without the mentalism/magic community as disclaimers. It seems that a preponderance of the magic community seethes when a mentalist fails to issue a strong disclaimer about his alleged abilities.

They should find a better outlet for their energies.

On the oft-repeated 1996 TV special, *Hidden Secrets of Magic*, the big closer was Lance Burton being "buried alive" in a casket, hands and feet shackled, under six feet of dirt. For his last words before the stunt began, he looked solemnly into the camera and warned viewers not to try a similar stunt because, "If you do, you will die."

Interspersed throughout the show were scenes of the history of the "challenge" and Lance talking about the need to fight fear and panic. In all ways, this was presented in the same fashion as Blaine's ice stunt and Copperfield's Tornado of Fire; that is, a legitimate stunt, which, while exceedingly difficult, could be mastered with proper training, preparation, and know-how.

But, unlike the Blaine and Copperfield stunts, this was a true magic *trick*.

In this case, did Lance have a responsibility to let his audience know he never really was six feet under? Did the documentary-style build-up to the climax cross the line between reality and theater? Surely, for some viewers, it did, and they believed that a human can truly survive after being buried under six feet of topsoil.

But if we agree that Lance, in what was clearly a "magic" show, did no harm (and I don't think he did), then what harm can there ever be in a mentalist picking up the vibes, thoughts, feelings of his audience, *while on stage?*

It comes down to this: *the mentalist has no responsibility to either educate or enlighten.* His job, especially when he's being paid, is to *entertain* a group of people. Assuming no one in the audience alters the course of his or her life after viewing one of our shows— a valid assumption I make after decades in this field—what's the problem with not letting them know "this is a trick"?

Looking at it from the opposite point of view, I can think of little that might be gained by the use of a forceful disclaimer. You can spend hours carefully crafting your disclaimer, but I assure you, for most people, ten minutes later, and certainly the day after your performance, no one will remember the tiny slice of your time on stage devoted to setting the record straight. They just don't care. If you are amazing and they can't fathom any explanation, your disclaimer, delivered early in your show, carries as much weight as cotton candy on a windy day.

A forcefully voiced, unambiguous disclaimer slashes the mentalist's premise to shreds, and Extraordinary Moments ratchet down to become Tricks, or likely, mere Puzzles. The entertainment experience suffers, and no one gains.

On a Related Note...

The first time I attended a production at Monday Night Magic in Manhattan, noted writer and card magician Jamy Ian Swiss closed the show. He was preceded by Docc Hilford who did a "card reading" act. During Jamy's stint he threw in remarks that were sometimes sly, sometimes mocking remarks about the abilities of the "psychic" entertainer, none of which would surprise any reader of his prolific and erudite writings. Other mentalists in the audience posted what they saw in various online forums, which led many of my colleagues in the mentalist community to pounce on Swiss for his stance, saying, basically, "He was a jerk to have done that."

They're wrong.

He has the right to say anything he wants. As a performer, the moment he takes the stage, he is free to offer his view of the world, because that, in part, is what an artist does. *Any* artist—graphic, musical, magical, or otherwise. He shares his vision. If his vision mocks, satirizes, inflames, or exalts, well, that's part of theater.

From Aeschylus to Albee, theatrical experiences attempt to educate, elucidate, poke fun at authority, question belief systems. A drama professor of mine back at Hofstra continually told us, "Anything is acceptable in theater, except boredom."

If Jamy Ian Swiss, or anyone else, chooses to alienate a particular performer (or type of performer) for what he sees as a larger good, we have to accept it. You don't have to agree, but when it's your turn to step onstage, that's the time when you can share *your* vision.

Mental Magic

Aside from disclaimers, another raging discussion among mentalists is the "mentalism vs. mental magic" controversy. In general, mental magic uses more props. Also, the plots in mental magic tend to be more convoluted. Mental magic straddles a netherworld—not quite pure mentalism, yet a step removed from traditional magic.

The best of the working mentalists use only the most innocent of props: "invisible props." Invisible in the sense that the audience barely notices their existence—paper, pencils, ordinary tables, books. Mental magic uses items that more overtly draw attention to themselves—unusual stands, clocks, bags, boxes—and as such, performers in this category have to work harder to establish credibility. I won't go into a long discussion of this here; I just want to point out the pitfall of choosing this approach as opposed to the more bare-bones presentations.

Magic dealers sell mental magic. You need to refer to books to learn the purer strains of mentalism.

Brown and McCambridge

British mentalist Derren Brown is little known outside the United Kingdom, but beginning with the first of his television specials in December, 2000, he became the Next Big Thing in mentalism. It appears that he may become more widely known around the time this book achieves publication, so a few words seem appropriate.

To get right to the point: his several TV specials in the U.K. represent nothing less than a sea change in the way mentalism is presented on television. For those who have already seen them, yes, they are direct descendents of David Blaine's specials, that is, both men work their miracles anywhere and everywhere, *except* on a stage. But where Blaine accomplishes many Extraordinary Moments in front of the camera, Brown manages to pull off hour-long shows that hold *nothing but* Extraordinary Moments! The cumulative effect is a paradigm-shifting, mind-altering experience for the viewer.

As this book entered its final stages of writing, Gerry McCambridge's NBC television network special, "The Mentalist," began production. It is expected to be the first of several prime-time specials he'll be doing for NBC. For those of us who know Gerry well, that's a thrill. He deserves his coming success, and I can report there is no question that he is fully capable of delivering solid, powerful entertainment to a live audience.

Prepare yourself for the inevitable wave of Derren Brown and Gerry McCambridge knock-off performers. But that's just fine. These two performers will take mentalism to new heights, and best of all, from my perspective, is that I know their work cannot easily be duplicated by others.

*   *   *

The mentalist suggests or reaffirms what the mind can do; he sells the *possibility* that strange things are afoot in the universe. All leading mentalists manage to do that without resorting to what had previously been known as "showmanship." By allowing their miraculous "effects" to speak for themselves, the performer shines brightly.

Chapter 17
Dealing with Spectators

Singers, dancers, musicians, and most comedians can run through their complete act in front of an empty room and then do exactly the same performance in front of a packed house. We can't. Most magicians, and all mentalists, interact with members of the audience. They become parts of our show, often important parts, and that's why we need to conscientiously consider the ways we treat them.

Or mistreat them.

The one time I visited the now-shuttered but once-enjoyable Caesar's Magical Empire in Las Vegas, the magician working the close-up room was a name known to all who regularly read the magic magazines. Not much about that show remains in my ever-depleting memory, but I do clearly recall this: he had two spectators with him at the table, and *he never asked for their names!*

They were props, no more important to him than any card, coin, or sponge ball he used that night.

To me, it felt as though he had insulted those two civilians, who were nice enough to risk embarrassment by accepting his request to sit next to him for his entire set. Don't forget, volunteers have no idea what the "professional entertainer" has in store for them. They are doing you a favor, a big favor, by offering themselves up for... what? They don't know.

This performer not only failed to ask their names, he never thanked them for being part of his show, never acknowledged their presence in any sincere way. That attitude muted, I'm certain, the audience's reaction to him.

Unless you set something up prior to the show, your volunteers have no idea that they will be in front of an audience. Those people are your guests. Treat them as guests, never as props to be manhandled.

When you meet a person socially, you extend your hand with a smile and say, or imply with your body language, "I'm pleased to meet you." On stage, no one is there to introduce you to your participants, so you must ask for their names. Not to do so sends a signal to the more socially conscious in the audience that either you don't care about your guests, you consider yourself more important than them, or your mama never taught you basic social niceties. In any of those cases, you lose.

If possible, let the volunteers get the laughs. Laughter is laughter, regardless of its source, and all laughter is a desired reaction. Plus, you look even better by allowing the rookies to share the spotlight with you.

The audience will judge you by the way you treat their colleagues, even if they are colleagues only in the sense of being fellow audience members.

Asking for Volunteers

When I was a young teenager, I read a book on doing magic for children. (The author, I believe, was Bert Easley.) One piece of simple advice from that book stayed with me forever, advice that too many performers seem to have missed:

Never announce, "I need a volunteer."

Say that at a kids' show—up to and including college kids—and you'll be swamped with volunteers. (But at least the eighteen-year-olds won't all run up at once and tug on your pants.)

When performing for adults, one of two things happens if you declare, "I need a volunteer."

No one volunteers, which leads to an awkward moment as everyone avoids eye contact with you, hoping you'll choose some other unlucky soul. Or you do get some hands raised, and you realize too late that those people are the ones you least want sharing the stage with you.

When you announce that you need someone to join you on stage, the kind folks staring up at you have no idea what is about to happen. (And frankly, at some shows I wonder, "Why would any sane adult offer themselves up for what appears to be certain humiliation?")

When doing magic or mentalism, it's vitally important that *you* choose the "volunteers." (This does not apply to hypnosis shows where, for ethical and perhaps legal reasons, it's imperative that everyone knows the volunteers came up of their own volition.) You want to Control Every Moment. If you ask for a volunteer and no hand goes up, the audience at that moment controls you!

Be wary of the various methods for randomly choosing volunteers, such as tossing a paper ball into the audience. That's excellent for those occasions when you simply want a piece of information which all would agree is impossible for you to know beforehand, (for example, "Please call out a number between one and fifty") but it's a poor idea for selecting volunteers to join you on stage. Again, it places control out of your hands, and you might quickly find yourself regretting the capriciousness of the toss.

Once you've made your request for a spectator to join you, *do not accede to any request that you* "pick someone else." If you do cave in, the next person will say the same thing. And the next. Instead, assure your chosen spectator that she is perfect for what is about to take place, then say something along the lines of, "I guarantee you'll feel comfortable and you'll have a great time! Come on up... it'll be fun!"

The skill of choosing the right person develops over time. In general, the person who desperately wants to join you on stage is the last person you want.

Please and Thank You

Please, say "please" when asking that something be done.

And "thank you" at its completion.

Thank you.

If only it were that simple. The fact is, too many performers forget common courtesy during a performance. They order this woman to "stand here," and that man to "hold this... higher." The audience judges you by the way you treat their comrades, so be mindful of your manners and respectful at all times. That is, unless your name is The Amazing Jonathan, in which case you can do pretty much whatever you please.

213

Clear Directions

People's minds wander throughout the show, even when they are on stage as participants. Actually, *especially* when they are on stage. They are nervous and easily distracted.

When giving instructions to your volunteers, look right at them. If you are not establishing eye contact with each person on stage, *rest assured that the verbal message you are sending is not being received.*

Be clear. Be precise. Be direct and to the point. If the success of your next effect depends on the volunteer carrying through on your instructions, repeat the instructions in a slightly different way.

The most important advice I can give you about this subject is: *Look for, or ask for, nods of comprehension.*

Performers who ignore this step will see their tricks get screwed up from time to time. Guaranteed.

When dealing with a group on stage, always say something to the effect of, "Is everyone clear about that?" *Do not proceed* until you have received clear and unambiguous affirmative responses from everyone.

Talking to Spectators

From a stagecraft point of view, when you have spectators on stage with you, you cannot talk to them face to face, the way you would in a social setting. You must converse while considering the needs of the larger target of your words, the audience as a whole. That's why you must angle *both yourself and the volunteer* so that, while she can plainly see and understand you, the audience does not feel left out.

Proper positioning:

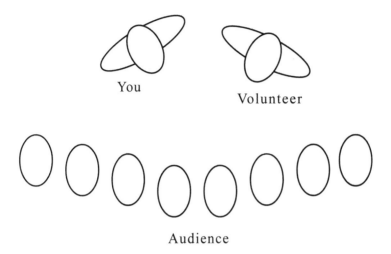

Never either of these positionings:

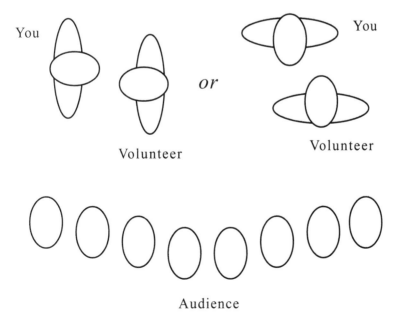

Listening

Magicians and mentalists need to develop good listening skills when dealing with non-performers on stage.

"Hi, what's your name?"

"Neil Armstrong."

"Glad to meet you, Neil. Where ya' from?'

"Well, I'm based in Houston."

"Fantastic. What do you do there?"

"I'm a retired astronaut."

"Great. Now would you please verify that these cards are thoroughly mixed?"

Far-fetched? I have seen something close to this take place, and I know it happens frequently because performers a) are nervous, b) are focused on the mechanics of the trick, and c) have never developed a "listening" attitude.

Listen to your guests on stage. You will look foolish if it becomes clear to the audience that you ask questions and don't really hear the responses. Listen. And react.

Like I Said, Listen. And React.

Were you listening to me?

Dennis Franz, Emmy-winning star of *NYPD Blue*, told *TV Guide* why he admired Jackie Gleason:

"I remember seeing the movie 'Gigot' on television where he played a mute; he just showed so much expression in his face. I think that's when I learned the importance of listening... by watching that performance. Most actors want to talk all the time. I learned you don't have to talk, but you always have to listen. I realized he wasn't saying anything, but he was breaking my heart."

Your reaction to whatever is said or done guides the audience's reaction. An extreme example: when something funny happens on stage, Kreskin, in my opinion, wildly *overreacts* by erupting into a spasm of limb-flailing laughter, but nonetheless his reaction increases the laughter in the audience.

That type of reaction will be more helpful to your success than if you simply hear words and proceed. The words a spectator says must register with you, and we in your audience must know that they did. Don't let it appear that you are a machine, programmed to say the same words regardless of the context. React when appropriate.

And listen to your audience. Marc Salem told me that the best director he has is the audience itself. They let you know what's working, and what needs improvement. Stay alert for those intensely important clues.

Touching

Politeness on stage (and you're "on stage" anytime you're in front of an audience of any size) extends beyond the basic "Please" and "Thank You" boundaries. The new consciousness of male/female relationships and "personal space" requires more sensitivity than was exhibited by many of our predecessors. Touch another person only when absolutely necessary, and restrict those touches to the universally accepted safe zones.

Dismissing Spectators

Always verbally thank your assistants. Always. Even when they screwed up (we've already discussed "fault"). And always with a smile.

Generally you want to shake the hand of anyone who's assisted you on stage, although there may be times when to do so breaks the rhythm of the moment. You should also ask the audience to acknowledge volunteer assistants, again assuming that it fits the pacing of the routine. But avoid a grandiose "C'mon folks, *let's hear it for them!*" if your volunteers haven't done all that much. Save your big requests for audience applause if and when a volunteer truly helps the show reach a high point.

Just as you may have helped people walk up onto the stage, when appropriate, assist them as they make their way back.

Prepare for Problems

Before you step out onto the stage, be sure to consider all the possible problems you might encounter when dealing with spectators:

• Difficult access to the stage.

• The audience is too old or too young.

• You need to borrow something (a bill, coin, ring, handkerchief), but no one has it.

• They don't understand you, due either to hearing or language problems.

• They screw you up, intentionally or otherwise.

Have alternative strategies immediately ready for all of these situations.

Chapter 18
During the Show

This is it. This is where all the planning and rehearsal hit the road.

In this chapter, more than any other, what you will read evolved directly from in-the-audience note-taking I've done over several years. This is my strongest real-world advice. I'm not there when the performer chooses material or writes scripts or rehearses, but I *can* comment on what finally makes it to public display.

So, please read and proceed with care: although I comment only on those potholes and slippery slopes that affect large segments of our art, it's prudent for you to assume *everything* in this chapter began by seeing you, or someone similar to you, perform.

Also, these opinions stem solely from seeing shows given by pros or the most highly advanced amateurs. (If I wrote about performance errors made at magic club shows, I'd be writing into the third millennium).

Your Opening Moments

It's useful to think of first moments in front of the audience as a job interview. You want to be on your best behavior, to impress from the start. Make friends with the audience. Let them know, by your smile, your words, and your body language, that standing there in front of them pleases you immensely.

"It's an honor for me to be here with you." You won't necessarily say that with words; you project that feeling with your face and body.

And you project that attitude *no matter what*. Improperly set stage lights, a microphone that cuts out, waiters still noisily clearing dishes despite your explicit instructions that they be off the floor once you begin—none of these can be allowed to impinge upon your opening moments.

Remember, *they don't care*. The audience doesn't care about the performer's problems, so to point out anything that's not to your liking, especially in the opening moments, serves no useful purpose and reflects poorly on you. Therefore, as I suggested previously, you walk out with an air of confidence, ready to smile and greet your awaiting audience.

You project a more commanding presence if you don't start talking the second your mouth is in range of the microphone. Wait at least two or three seconds before you do or say anything at all. Anchor yourself. Let the audience focus on you.

Then get started immediately. That should be no problem because:

- You made certain that all your props were in place before you walked out.
- The microphone is where you expected it to be, and the mike stand has been adjusted to the proper height.
- If you're using a clip-on microphone, you're already certain it's been turned on.

Ewww! Gag Me with a Spoon

If your goal is to be a man of mystery, why start with a weak gag? When I see a performer early in his set ask a spectator,

"Do you know what word I'm thinking of?"

"No."

"That's correct!"

I know it's going to be a weak act.

Similarly for a long joke. Unless you are certain the story *kills*, save it for later. Leisurely openings worked on the Chautauqua circuit, but no longer. In the age of MTV, when nothing seems to stay on the screen for more than two seconds, people need stimulation quickly, so get something concrete started within your first thirty seconds.

Take a moment to get comfortable on stage, then let them know what you are about. You might start with a strong trick, or a quick story or joke. But don't dawdle. The audience grants you a very short honeymoon before they mentally decide whether this is a relationship they care to pursue.

"Strong," by the way, does not necessarily mean a knock-'em-dead routine; it could be anything that you know from experience works to get their attention *and* establish your character.

About Face!

Banquet performers face obstacles not found in other situations: the clinking of glasses and silverware, wait staff delivering and clearing food, and one other particularly dangerous hazard... people sitting at round tables. Some in the audience are facing you; some have their backs to you.

When performing at a banquet, or any situation where people are sitting at round tables, acknowledge the fact that you cannot see everyone and they cannot easily see you.

Do not allow yourself to perform for backs of heads!

If you do, they *will* talk during your show, and that hurts you. Control the situation!

After a very brief time on stage—no more than a few minutes—say something along the lines of:

"Ladies and gentlemen, if you are not already facing this way, please take a moment right now to turn your chairs so you can see me and I can see you.

No stiff necks allowed! The whole show happens up here. Trust me, I've seen this before."

Failing to make this request is a major mistake.

You may have asked the emcee to take on this duty prior to your introduction. Sometimes that suffices, sometimes not. If not, take matters into your own hands.

Do You See What I See?
Do You Hear What I Hear?

You've just had a woman in the audience choose a card and you instruct her to "Show the card to everyone."

Did everyone see the card? *Are you certain?*

You need to presume that every person watching wants see and hear everything (whether it's true or not). When I'm the audience and I cannot see the selected card, my attenti starts to wilt. You've experienced the same feeling.

Therefore, when a card is selected and you ask that it be shown the audience, *you* must ensure that everyone sees that card. Do forget, you are Controlling Every Moment, and you lose control if yc spectator does not wholly follow your instructions. Simply asking, "L you all see the card?" might be enough. This applies to any effect which you have asked that something be displayed by a civilian. L folks, for the most part, lack a sense of theater. They talk softly a they won't make their movements expansive, so you must keep yc eyes and ears attuned to the situation.

Recently I saw James Mapes, a major-league sta hypnotist, neglect this basic tenet. During one of the strong parts of his program, he has a woman write on an overhe projector as he "regresses" her to age twelve and then age si It's fascinating to see how her writing changes. Or it wou have been. She had inadvertently moved the projector, and while she and Jim talked about what she was writing on t transparency, those of us in the audience of more than o thousand were clueless... he never looked up to see what were seeing, which was just shadow!

When I did my Psychic Entertainers Associati "Performance Workshops," this type of problem was the fl that I needed to point out the most often. These glitches can avoided if you accept and work toward this truth:

Anything of any importance that happens during your sh must be seen and heard by everyone.

When cards are selected, when locks are examined, wh you address anyone on stage with you or in the audience, wh an item is to be displayed:

Be aware, be aware, be aware of what the audience sees and hear

Play everything to the widest audience possible. The ba row is as important as the front row, because you never kn who's sitting where.

Some performers seem to know this instinctively. In 2002, I attended a lecture given by Joshua Jay. At one point, he was demonstrating one of his devastating moves with cards and realized some in the back of the room were having difficulty seeing his hands. What did he do? He jumped up on the table! He controlled the situation in a way I've seen few others do, including pros with many more years of performing experience. And this happened when he was still many months away from attaining the legal right to order a beer!

You Control Every Moment by being aware of everything around you.

Rise to the Occasion

Audience participation is a good thing. But it leads to a conundrum when you're about to interact with a person in the audience. If that spectator remains seated, you immediately risk losing the attention of those who cannot see him or her (which essentially is everyone not within a few feet of the person). In general, my advice is for you to ask that person to stand up. (Too many performers seem to think that if they can see the face of the person standing, we all can.) On the other hand, when a person stands in the audience, he or she is blocking the view of at least a few, and perhaps many other people.

If you control who is going to participate, choose people as far back into the audience as you feel you can comfortably manage. How often have we seen performers continually choose and interact with people in the front? Spread the joy around the room!

An important tip: whenever you have someone stand for more than a short moment, move around on stage. Walk closer to the person or, for dramatic effect, walk to the opposite side of the stage. In either case, audience members whose view had been blocked now will be able to see you. The longer a person is standing, the more important it becomes that you, the true center of attention, shift position on stage.

If you are dealing with people down front (perhaps chosen by some random method), and what they say ought to be heard by all, you might ask them to "Please turn around and say that to everyone."

And finally, if you must deal with someone for longer than perhaps a minute or two, it may be wiser simply to have that person join you on stage.

Avoid Dead Time

You seek to Eliminate Weak Spots from your act, and there's nothing weaker than dead time.

You impose dead time on your audience whenever nothing is happening, or something is happening that fails to hold the audience's attention (caution: a tension-inducing dramatic pause is *not* a nothing moment). Cards being counted, numbers being added, a spectator searching for a $20 bill that you've asked to borrow... all are moments that tend to be less than riveting.

You *can* incorporate these moments into your show, provided something else occurs concurrently. A recap of the action may do the job:

- "I want to remind you that these people were all selected randomly."
- "She could have named *any* number, and she said twenty-four."
- "The locks were provided by the Suffolk County Police Department, and then thoroughly checked by five audience members."

Or you might sidestep dead time with a running commentary of the action, provided that the commentary holds your audience's interest by offering some new information:

- "I couldn't help but notice that your handbag seems to have been packed for, what, a weekend at the beach?"
- "While he counts, you'll notice the graceful manner with which he handles the cards. The result of years of dorm-room poker, no doubt."

The best performers know that something must be happening even when "nothing" is happening. That something can be as simple as looking out into the audience... purposefully. Comedians have used this tactic with great success for as far back as their voices have been recorded. When Jack Benny stopped talking and slowly raised his hand to his chin, that was his signature "nothing" that signaled what was going on his mind, and it got a laugh. When Jerry Seinfeld rhetorically asks, "Who *are* these people?", there's a laugh, followed by a pause as we watch him consider his own question. When a mentalist peers into the audience to find from whence the thought he's receiving emanates, "nothing" is happening, but there is drama in the moment, *provided the audience knows he is in full control.*

If the audience suspects, even for a moment, that the pause is happening because uncertainty has crept into the routine, they will start to lose their connection to the entertainer. Your antidote to those poisonous moments is meticulous preparation—along with your steely-jawed promise to yourself: *never lose control.*

Careful Where You Step

Every time you leave the stage, or the "stage" area, you risk losing your hold on your audience. A few performers (mentalist Marc Salem, for one) thrive on getting down and dirty with their spectators by moving among them. And certainly it's not an issue for two-person acts such as the Evasons, which has Jeff roaming the audience (and keeping up a constant flow of fast-paced chatter—with a wireless handheld microphone) while lovely Tessa locks the focus on the stage.

But more often, leaving the stage backfires. Step into the audience where I can't see you, and suddenly I don't care about you. Why should I? You obviously don't care about me. If I am forced to strain to see or hear the action, negative vibes are setting in.

It comes back to being aware of everything the audience sees and hears.

225

Too many performers believe they are increasing audience-participation factor by descending into the audie when in fact they are boosting interest merely for those w happen to be sitting near the action. Others lose interest, *stay in control* by staying up where all can see and hear yo

Share, and Share Again

Every word you utter while in front of an audience sho matter and should move your act forward. If every word tr is important, then don't cheat anyone out of the pleasure hearing those words. Other than stage-whispers or words y intentionally say off-microphone, *say everything to the ent audience*, from the front to the last person in the back row. H mumbled asides make those who missed them feel left out.

Unless there is a clear reason for you to do so, don't t your back to the audience.

Be aware, too, that not every person in your audience hangs your every word. You need to reinforce key points. So, for example you showed that the cards were all different at the beginning of a l trick, you may want to show them again at the conclusion, especi if an obvious solution would be that "all the cards are the same."

If you can anticipate some of the "explanations" for y miracles, and demolish them without sacrificing the impact the presentation, do so.

No "Thank you"

At the close of each trick, you may want to say, "Thank y very much." That's fine, but I believe that phrase should be u just once. As pointed out earlier, we strive to surprise. Repeat the "thank you very much" becomes repetitive since it off nothing new. You do not need to thank your audience after ev climax, but you do need to acknowledge the culmination of routine. With just a bit of thought, you can revise your script that the final words punch up the close: a true punch line.

You might use a recap ("I can't believe I found one card of thousands!") or some variation of an emphatic *"yes!"* to highlight the difficulty you managed to overcome (although actually saying the word "yes" is a bit hackneyed). If you have volunteers on stage with you, asking for applause to thank your assistants nicely closes the routine.

A quick Ronald Reagan-like bow of just your head signals "Thank you" without saying it.

Signing Off On Signing

On the day you read this sentence, thousands of magicians around the world, as part of a routine, will ask a spectator to sign something so they can prove that the object displayed at the beginning of the routine is that same object shown at the climax.

It's time to rethink that process.

When you ask to have a bill or a card signed, you set up a challenge.

"Uh-oh," the spectator reasons, "I better keep an eye on this bill because he's gonna do *something* sneaky with it."

If you do have a card, bill, or any other object signed, you have three choices from an entertainment perspective:

- Make the process of signing part of the entertainment (not an easy task), or

- Keep up the patter by having something witty or useful to say to the signer or observers, or

- Stand back and let the magic come to the fore, that is, go for maximum impact by using minimum "showmanship" à la Blaine.

In theory, the third choice should be the easiest one. The very fact that you want the object signed signals that this unfolding demonstration has serious mystical qualities. In other words, it's a great trick. ("Lordy, lordy, how did my card get into the envelope inside his wallet?") But it's also the most likely tactic to result in dead time. This option works only when your target is a highly charged dramatic moment.

227

Always ask yourself, "Does the signing of the card or bill truly add to the final impact of the routine?" In many routines, the signing ceremony adds little, while slowing down the proceedings.

I previously alluded to one example of this problem in the Case Study for *Ripped & Restored.* Here's another example, this time from Jon Allen's *Ghost* routine on his *Spectators Don't Exist* video: He borrows a $20 bill, has it signed, and this is what ensues:

- Dead time while the elderly man meticulously writes his first and last names.
- More dead time when he looks for, finds, and then replaces the cap of the pen.
- Still more dead time when Jon asks for the pen back.
- And sure enough, a few moments into the routine, the man turns to his wife and asks, "Is that the same bill?"

It's obvious why the man asked that: at the start, Jon set the routine up as some sort of "catch-me-if-you-can" challenge. Again, in the spectator's mind, *why else would he be required to sign a perfectly ordinary object?*

Then the routine gets on track and the bill jumps around quite magically, the bill is handed back, and the group of three applauds sincerely and appreciatively.

To most performers, that was a successful routine. And it was! But it could have been a bit smoother.

How different would the take-home memory be if that bill had not been signed? To my mind, not very. Paper currency is not supposed to hover in the air and dance inside a wine glass just inches from the spectators' faces.

The magic is this: Jon borrows a bill, crumples it up, drops it into a glass, and, untouched, it moves and eventually jumps through the air.

What difference does it make if *this* bill floats, or *that* bill? A floating, dancing, hopping bill is magic. Period. Asking the spectator to sign the bill sets up a needless challenge that adds nothing to the entertainment value of the routine. Plus, if you conclude by returning the bill, that, in itself, confirms its normalcy.

Yes, there are routines where the mystery grows appreciably by proving the coin, card, or bill you start with is the one you end with. Just be certain the incremental proof of your magical prowess does not diminish the entertainment value of the routine.

Let's look at this from the opposite point of view. We have a multitude of examples where gimmicked objects are not signed, yet the magic suffers not a whit. Mike Skinner's Ultimate Three-Card Monte uses specially printed cards, and all eyes burn those three cards for several minutes. Yet, according to Skinner, Bill Malone, Patrick Page, and others who feature this and similar routines, no one asks to examine the cards. Why? Because the routines are carefully constructed to give the audience the impression that they repeatedly see all the fronts and backs.

Suppose someone comes up with a method to accomplish those identical Three-Card Monte effects *with borrowed cards*. It's certain that *some* magicians would have the cards signed—to "prove" something. Would that strengthen the effect? No, signing would add nothing for a lay audience. (For magicians, yes. For normal people, no.)

Lastly, if you must have the object signed, initials deliver the same impact as a full signature and take less time.

Power Shifting

Transitions—the moments between tricks—suffer if they are not as well rehearsed as the tricks themselves. It's a problem endemic among amateurs, and some pros as well.

The actions and words that take your show from the climax of one effect to the opening of the next *are not afterthoughts!* What do you do with the card case/scissors/linking rings when you finish with each? Do you casually toss them aside? Is that the image you want? It might be, but *is* it? Or did you toss them aside because you never thought about what message that sends?

How do you pick up those props? Where are they? How do you get from one spot on stage to another? If you have not worked those answers out beforehand, you will pay the price during your show.

Whose Fault Is It, Anyway?

In an Internet mentalism forum, a performer posted a message about seeing a fellow performer who:

> *"... asked the person to open the book to any page and think of a word. When the mentalist divined the wrong word, the person said. 'Oh, you meant a word from the book?'"*

And then the writer berated the volunteer for his supposed stupidity.

In the service industry, the adage says, "the customer is always right." When something goes wrong in show biz, you'd better believe that the audience assumes "the performer is always at fault." *The facts don't matter.* The fault could have been totally beyond your control, but still *you* bear the blame. Performers all too often claim—as Shakespeare had Cassius say in *Julius Caesar*— that the fault lies somewhere other than within themselves.

In the case described above, two possible causes come to mind. He either picked the wrong person to help, or he failed to instruct clearly. Or both.

The instructions, as related in the anecdote ("open the book to any page and think of a word"), are not as clear as many magicians or mentalists believe. A nervous or confused spectator might think that you were going to do something else with the book—perhaps announce the page number stopped at, or describe pictures on the page.

Or, the spectator parsed the performer's instructions with literal exactness:

1. "Open the book to any page." *OK, I did that.*

2. "Think of a word." *OK, I'll think about, let's see ... my favorite sport ... "Baseball."*

Ta-da! The performer is screwed.

Then, too, an obstreperous spectator might deliberately exploit the ambiguity.

The solution is to foresee these scenarios and then script your words to head off problems. So, for example, in this case:

Please open the book to any page. Have you done that? Thank you. Now please let your eyes move over that page and then focus your gaze on just one of the words you see there..."

Having the attitude "it's always my fault" may seem slightly paranoid but it's an attitude a performer needs to cultivate internally. He must actively work toward solutions, rather than blaming the audience. A performer's attitude, when a moment doesn't go as planned, ought to be, "*I* could have done *something* to avoid that problem. What do I need to do next time to make it right?"

It's a masochistic mindset, but ultimately it leads to a higher level of success.

The temptation to blame someone or something else is *huge*. Don't give in to it. As magicians and mentalists, one skill we *must* possess is the ability to create clear verbal instructions that minimize possible misunderstanding. As a reasonable first step, avoid any routine that involves complex verbal instructions.

And always acknowledge, dear performer, that the fault lies not in our stars, but in ourselves.

When Bad Things Happen to Good Performers

And they will. The gods that decide who shall kill today (theatrically speaking, that is) and who shall melt into a puddle of flop sweat are notoriously capricious. Doves die, metal fatigues, cards drop, and non-English-speaking spectators come on stage to help you with your Add-a-Number. Disasters, major and minor, befall all performers eventually.

I recall a lecture given by Marvyn Roy (Mr. Electric). He regaled us with reminiscences of a glitteringly successful lifetime in show business, and he didn't shirk from sharing how, despite hours of careful preparation before each twelve-minute set, at one time or another everything that could go wrong, did.

Murphy's Law will subpoena you too one day. When it does:

Cut your losses. The sooner the better.

I have watched the quicksand of calamity suck performers down as they unwisely struggled to put things right. Don't let that happen to you! Instead, within moments of realizing that something has gone dreadfully wrong, move on. You might preface the transition with words along the lines of:

"Ladies and gentlemen, things aren't going as planned. Fortunately, I have..."

and advance *immediately* to your next routine.

What if the screw-up happens during your *final* routine? Same advice: cut the bit as soon as you realize it's beyond repair. Except now (and I'm assuming you don't have an alternative ending) you're going to rely on your charm to steer your ship back to port. A smile, perhaps a friendly shrug, a quick acknowledgment that "it's just one of those things," will Communicate Your Humanity, alleviate the tension, and help you reconnect with the audience. You've been successful in all else, and now you can still bring your show to a successful conclusion. At the soonest possible moment, return to your script and close the show, and once you do return to the script, *never acknowledge that anything went awry.*

They don't care.

Above all, when bad things happen, it's *never* anyone else's fault. Regardless of the actual cause of the misfortune, the entertainer can never blame the civilian or the backstage folks (well, actually you *can* dump on the knuckle-dragging doofusses who caused you harm... just not while you're still in front of the audience).

Smile, And the Whole World Smiles with You

Don't forget to smile as often as is practical throughout your time in front of an audience.

What happens in a social situation when you smile at someone? They smile back at you. Similarly, when you are on stage and you sincerely smile at the people watching you, they spontaneously smile.

Human beings feel happy when they smile, so anything you can do to induce smiles is a good thing. When people smile, their brains reflexively respond by thinking to themselves, "I'm having a good time!"

That works!

A Personal Entertainment Highlight:
Gil Eagles — The Q&A Act

I first met Gil Eagles in the Catskill Mountains, where we were two young mentalists competing against each other in the early 1970s. I was earning $75 a show and Gil, a few years my senior, was raking in a jealousy-inducing $125 per, and he often did seven or eight shows a week (this during a time when Gil was renting a Greenwich Village studio apartment for $80 a month)! As a budding mentalist, I had studied the texts about acts in which the audience writes questions, hidden from the performer's view, and the mystic gives out answers with startling accuracy. Most of those texts had been written in the 1930s and '40s and I was certain the hip audiences of the swinging '70s would scoff and snicker at any fool who tried to hold their attention with such antics.

Could I have been more wrong?

Over the years, I have audited Gil Eagles' show many times, in many venues, including colleges and high-end corporate gigs (Gil's list of *repeat* gigs is a highly representative sampling of the Fortune 500, always for big money, always plus first-class airfare and limo). There is never a moment when those around me are not zeroed in on the man onstage. As he apparently culls thoughts from random spots around the room while hopelessly blindfolded with silver dollars, tape, and cloth, bodies lean forward so that not a moment is missed. He evokes laughter without jokes, and amazes in ways having nothing to do with magic-text "tricks."

When he announces that he is going to answer just one more question, palpable disappointment invariably engulfs the room. Now, understand that Gil never gives out "psychic predictions" about any spectator's future. He answers questions by reflecting back information he knows about the present situation, yet in a manner that indicates some sort of extraordinary, unknowable knowledge. He does it with compassion, amazing skill, and of-the-moment humor. No other performer has perfected the

Question and Answer Act to this level, and I fear that, once Gil hangs up the blindfold for good, a piece of our craft will be permanently retired.

A Highlight within a Highlight: Removing the Blindfold

It's a nondescript moment. At least, it should be. No music plays, no magic or special effects of any kind take place, no stories are told... simply the necessary actions for concluding his performance. For almost thirty minutes he has stood before the audience, bereft of eye contact. Now he must remove the blindfold and remind all that his power of vision has been blocked beyond question.

He brings his face directly up to the microphone (handheld, of course, on a mike stand) and ever so slowly peels the white surgical tape down, the skin pulling away from his pliable face. As the r-r-r-ripping sound carries over the PA system, every set of eyes stares, transfixed. When finished, his hands, holding the blindfold paraphernalia, drop to his side. He blinks as his eyes adjust to the light, and he takes a small bow, really just a nod of the head. It's a non-theatrical (by traditional standards) climactic moment of high-level impact and there is never a sound in the audience while it's happening. An ovation breaks the silence, every time.

When the show is over, most often the meeting planner is immediately peppered with questions about, "When can we bring him back?"

By the way, as Gil (who went on to become a major-award-winning motivational speaker and who is semi-retired now) will happily tell you, his act today is exactly the same act he did in the Catskills for $125.

Can you say, "Practice makes perfect"?

Chapter 19
Closing the Show

In most cases, the final minute or two won't be remembered well by the audience, at least not the specifics. But these moments are intensely critical to your success. It's the *feeling* you impart to your audience *now* that can make or break you.

No matter what happened during your time on stage—even if you had props break, tricks fail, or jokes produce groans instead of laughs—as you close your show, your confidence in your abilities and your poise never falters. Never.

You are Superman, and Superman remains humble, gracious, *and in total control.*

Dominate the terrain, especially as you prepare to exit.

Last Man Standing

Building to a Climax for the close of your show is rarely a straight, clearly marked road. The difficulty of navigating that road can be seen in two consecutive email postings to an online forum in which I participate. An emerging mentalist asked questions, yet also, to my mind at least, indirectly answered them himself.

In the first email he wrote:

"I want my audience to feel SAFE enough to allow their fears and inhibitions to disappear and allow their inner child to surface and experience the same sense of play, wonder and involvement that a child felt at my magic show. Of course I want them to go home remembering me and telling their friends about me and the show. Of course I want better bookings at higher fees but beneath all that I want them to unlock their inner sense of wonder."

In the second posting, he pondered how to effectively close his show with a card memory routine that concludes with two spectators still on stage with him.

"So at the very end, when you should theatrically be alone to take your applause, you have to deal with thanking and dismissing two helpers."

Here is what I wrote in response:

By wanting to close the show at the moment of the climax of the "trick" you are putting all your faith in the power of the trick (or routine). But if you truly believe what you said in the first posting, the audience by that time loves YOU. Therefore, dismiss your two helpers with a round of applause, then bask in the glow the audience will be feeling toward you. With a few choice words, recap the wonders you brought to their lives for a brief moment, and, if done correctly, all the focus will be back on your smile, and your charm, and on you as you thank the audience for their attention and take your well-earned bow.

He was stone cold right about one instinct: unless you work with an assistant, it's imperative that you are the only person on stage at the finale.

Standing Ovations

An ovation is sustained applause. A *standing* ovation is the royal flush of show business, the summa cum laude acknowledgment from an audience, and every performer craves it.

I feel squeamish offering advice on this subject, for, in theory, you either deserve an ovation—standing or otherwise—or you don't.

That said, as with so much else in show business, there are tricks of the trade for the close of your show, and there are things you can do to boost your chances of getting the people on their feet. I've seen some tactics so blatant they make me cringe, even when they are meant to be funny—for example, playing patriotic music (with or without a waving flag), or telling a story about "my sick young son back home who will ask me when I kiss him in his bed tonight, 'Daddy, did the nice people stand up at the end of your show?'"

Don't do that. Please.

Instead, structure your act so that you have *as thrilling a climax as possible.* I know, that's easy to write, difficult to do, but it's paramount.

Assuming you *do* have a strong climax:

- Don't rush off the stage. Take a bow and stay there for as long as the sound of the applause is peaking. (Once you hear the slightest diminishment of sound, make your exit.)

- As you come up from your bow (*caution:* what you are about to read borders on cheesy when done poorly; use with discretion), extend your arms at your side, palms turned toward the ceiling. In other words, it's the motion you would make if you were to actually signal the audience to stand. You don't make the full motion, you just start it. Your hands may move perhaps *an inch or two* without being obvious.

- If one or two people do stand, look right at them, extend your arms toward them, and say, or at least mouth the words, "Thank *you!*" These actions draw the attention of the rest of the audience to your biggest fans, and usually more will join the ovation.

During a discussion of the Big O with my friend, Ted Karmilovich, Jr. (one of the most important innovators of practical mental effects since Annemann), he mentioned that he sometimes feels embarrassed when people start to stand for an ovation. I recall the same feeling from early in my career, the feeling that somehow it's not sincere or perhaps not even deserved. The truth is, how well your show plays on any given night is not a reliable indicator of how the applause will go at the end, so you may in fact see people rising and applauding after what you felt was a mediocre performance. Fight that I-don't-deserve-this feeling!

A standing ovation is more than ego gratification; it's good business. When someone who wasn't at the show asks a friend, "How was he? Any good?," the person who did attend, presumably not a professional critic and who might otherwise stumble over an accurate summation, has been provided a shorthand answer: "Yeah, he was good. He got a standing ovation!" Nothing further need be said.

Section VII

◄ POSTSCRIPT ➤

"Additional information
appended to a manuscript."

Chapter 20
After the Show

The Spin Cycle

Invariably, when I happen to be present at a function for which a professional walk-around magician or mentalist has been hired, friends or relatives ask me, "Is this guy good?" My internal voice answers, "Well, you just saw him. What do *you* think?" But my socially acceptable voice says, "Sure. He's excellent." (Happily, most of the pros are, in fact, good to excellent).

They walk away feeling vindicated that their own impressions were correct.

Please don't underestimate the power of "spin." After every political debate the spin doctors rush onto the airwaves to tell us what we *really* saw and heard, and sometimes *their* messages can have more impact than that of the spinnee.

Similarly, after each of your performances, people approach you. They want to talk about you and what they just witnessed. Inside the privacy of your head you may be thinking that a couple of bits didn't "kill" nearly as well as they usually do, and you might want to tell them so. Or maybe, because of your innate humility, you want to downplay that "you-are-a-god" look in their eyes.

Don't. Allow each spectator to brew his or her own exalted recollection of your performance. *Help it along.* Spin their memories toward the highlights that worked especially strongly. If they happen to have caught you on an "off" night, you gain nothing by telling anyone, "Thanks, but most nights it's even better!" (I used to say this frequently. And stupidly. Gil Eagles straightened me out.)

Your spectators' final encounters with you may well be the moments they remember the longest. Buff those memories up to the brightest possible sheen. Here are a few techniques:

- When they recall a moment they clearly enjoyed, help them mentally replay the best parts. "Remember when Susan saw that *she* was holding the five dollar bill? She shrieked!" (Don't tell them you see that reaction 90% of the time.)

- Play off their comments with remarks about how *you* were blown away by someone's reaction. "Did you see the look on Fred's face when he...?" Let them think they were privileged to be present at a singularly riotous or special performance, one that impressed even you, the seasoned performer.

- Look for opportunities to praise the volunteers. "Wasn't it just fantastic the way Chloe...?"

- If possible, relate what they saw to a prestigious situation. "When I did that for the mayor, he dropped his drink!"

The entertainment process takes place before you walk on stage, and continues for as long as anyone thinks or talks about you.

Your "show," your performance, encompasses every moment you have contact with an audience member. From the time you arrive on the scene until your final exit—out the door—you are "on." Anything you say can and will be used against you in the court of public opinion, and you have no lawyer to intervene on your behalf. Projecting the best image is your sole responsibility.

Perception is reality. This is true in much of life, and especially in entertainment, where facts mean little and emotions rule. Before, during, and after your show, encourage the perception that, yes, you *are* good. Yes, you are a kind of Superman. Do it gently, subtly, and graciously, but do it.

If the situation arises, and *if* you are totally comfortable and confident in your material, performing informally after your show extends and enhances the entertainment experience. If executed expertly, it's a strong and wise professional tactic. Your hosts will feel that you've exceeded their highest expectations, and their opinions of you will glow even brighter. Just be sure—absolutely certain—that you "leave 'em wanting more." You can erase hours of goodwill by overstaying your welcome just a few minutes.

The Postmortem

I'm about to give you one of the most important suggestions in this book, an insight into the entertainment business that served me well over the years:

On the drive home, *turn off the radio.*
And the CD and cassette player.

That one simple action, repeated consistently, will yield more dividends to your success than pounds of magic books.

Instead of listening to depressing news or someone else's music, think about *your* show. Make a concentrated effort to mentally replay as much of your time on stage as possible. What worked? What didn't? Did you come up with a clever ad-lib that could be used in the future?

This stuff is gold! To let it evaporate into the ether is a sin and a waste.

Which leads to a second suggestion: buy a micro-cassette (or digital) recorder, and keep it in your car's glove compartment. As you go over your show in your mind, record your impressions.

A day or two later, when you have a chance to listen to the recording, I guarantee one of two things will happen—much of what you recorded will be incomprehensible or so abbreviated that you have no idea what brilliant message you tried to give yourself. Or, if you do understand your message, it will lead you to say out loud, "What the hell was I thinking?"

That's OK. In the hour or two immediately following your show, your adrenaline is still pumping, your senses are at full alert, and your understanding of what happened on stage is at its most focused and fresh. Some of these self-directed notes will sound brilliant a week later, some won't. Either way, don't waste these opportunities to examine and reflect.

Chapter 21

And, in the end...

We are all teachers and we are all students. We all learn from each other. We're all in this together.

That's not poetic fluff. Despite more than four decades of study, put me in a room with any magician past the neophyte stage, and within a reasonable time he will show me something new. A new trick, or a wrinkle on an old one—it's certain he knows something useful to me.

In what other art would that be true? Few, if any. It's just one more reason we find magic to be permanently and continually exciting.

*   *   *

Doing tricks does not make you a magician. And being a magician does not make you an entertainer.

A six-year-old boy can be taught to put a coin in a small box, close the drawer, wave his hand over the box and show that the coin has vanished. He is not a magician. A twelve-year-old girl who seeks out and reads magic books and who practices her presentations with deliberate thoughtfulness *is* a budding magician. A forty-year-old man who knows hundreds of card tricks but never makes eye contact with the spectators is a magician, but not an entertainer. Only by combining tricks with entertainment skills does one become a magical entertainer.

*   *   *

In the 1960s, as I went through my hippie phase, I taught myself to play guitar. During that time I visited a cousin, a boy a few years younger than myself, who was learning the instrument. Unlike me, however, he was taking lessons. As I showed him a few licks I had been working on, he stopped me and said, quite seriously, "you're not supposed to..."

Not supposed to? In music? Since I had never taken formal lessons, I had no idea there were "rules." I've often thought about that conversation.

247

Neither of us studied guitar with the goal of joining an ensemble. It was merely an outlet, a fun way of expressing something we felt, of finding and making a joyful noise. If I successfully communicated to my listeners, how could there be a "not supposed to"?

The artist discovers new art by ignoring the not-supposed-to's. Or by pushing the limits of the supposed-to's. We can never achieve originality if we walk only on the path others have carefully trod before us. Sometimes we have to risk stepping on a mine.

The artist awakens—or re-awakens—something dormant within us. New hope, curiosity, joy of life—these are the currency of the artist and the entertainer. The artist raises our sights to new possibilities, and he often accomplishes it by doing things he's "not supposed to."

*　*　*

In this book, you have advice distilled from my years as a performer along with concentrated study of other performers. Now, as we draw to a close, I want to recap the themes and concepts that will keep you in control and confident when you stand before audiences in service of your art. If you consistently drive toward the points listed below, performing excellence and maximum entertainment will be yours.

Above all, Have Fun!

Continuously strive to **Raise Your Level.** Where you do rank among your peers? Work to move up in the rankings.

When you are in front of an audience, **Every Moment Counts.** You want to present a seamless flow of riveting entertainment.

They don't care about you; they care about their own entertainment experience.

Videotape yourself! You will never reach your fullest potential until you see yourself as others see you.

When possible, move up the **Hierarchy of Mystery Entertainment:**

1. Puzzle
2. Trick
3. Extraordinary Moment

Use your personality and presentation skills to lever Puzzles into Tricks and Tricks into Extraordinary Moments.

Target your words with precision toward the most-valued **Reactions:**
1. Rapt Attention
2. Laughter
3. Astonishment

Build your act on **The Six Pillars of Entertainment Success.**

1. Master Your Craft. You cannot achieve success without total dominance of your material. Accept that the hard way is actually the easy way.

2. Communicate Your Humanity. Tell me who you are. Show me you care about me. Make me care more about *you* than your props.

3. Capture the Excitement. Which parts of your routines are trivial? Which stand out and will be remembered a week later? Something special happens in every magic trick. Find it. Emphasize it. Why should I spend a slice of my life watching you?

4. Control Every Moment. Be Superman in front of your audience. You cannot let the minds of your audience wander.

5. Eliminate Weak Spots. Remember that *everything* you do in front of an audience either enhances the entertainment or detracts from it. Every moment must have a purpose.

6. Build to a Climax. Invest extra time, effort, and creativity into delivering the absolute strongest close.

Nail your climax!

* * *

I have to assume that, once this book is published, I will lose the relative anonymity I've "enjoyed" in the world of magic (whether that's good or bad remains to be seen), and that some readers may want to communicate with me. So I make this offer. If you care to, let me know what you think about all this. You can email me at maxent@ken-weber.com. I will read your message carefully, but please don't be offended if I don't respond. First, I'm lazy about doing things I don't absolutely need to do. Second, I'm busy running my business and trying to be a good family man, friend, and neighbor. And third, did I mention I'm lazy?

*   *   *

"And, in the end, the love you take is equal to the love you make." So say the Beatles. So say I. The love you radiate to your audience reflects itself back on you. It's a great and noble feeling.

I want you to bask in that glory.

By intent, references in this book to my personal act have been few. As we conclude, allow me to relate the high point of my time on stage. The high point, that is, from the perspective of my eyes looking out at the audience. It has nothing to do with an explosive climax or the successful execution of a difficult routine.

It happens toward the end of my full evening program. The show starts relaxed and low key, gradually building in pace until reaching the final, somewhat frenzied moments. After I have spent from ninety minutes to two hours on stage with various volunteers, facing my audience of as many as two thousand, I abruptly slow things down.

They entered as strangers, the room vast and cold, the back rows distant. Now the room has warmed and the walls have pulled in closer. We are no longer strangers. They know me, and my interactions with many of them have made us, if not friends, at least acquaintances. Connections have been established.

With perhaps three minutes remaining in my program, I drop the microphone (handheld, of course) to my side, and, for the first time I speak directly to the audience, my voice now pure and unfiltered by technology.

With all eyes focused on me, and using the voice projection techniques I learned in my acting classes at Hofstra, I send my unamplified words (a minor joke) hurtling into the vast space beyond the front edge of the stage. After a second or two, I see the people in the farthest seats respond.

I do it because, within the context of the show, I'm *pretending* I don't want certain people on stage to hear what I'm saying. But to be truthful to you, I do it because I *can*. It's a thrill.

I control the audience. They trust me. I trust them. There are no extraneous sounds. As the lion tamer lowers the chair he had used to keep the beasts at bay, I lower the microphone and face my audience unshielded, unaided by any tool.

It's an exquisite moment of certainty.

I do it knowing that in just two or three minutes, as I take my bow and thank them, there will be enthusiastic applause.

Nothing "important" happens during that moment, nothing that will be remembered. Yet it's that brief slice of my show that gives me the highest level of personal satisfaction—twelve-year-old Kenny Weber, the asthmatic boy who began learning about show business in the basement of a Denver magic shop, has grown into a man who can transport a great throng of strangers into his made-up world.

As I write this, my evolution from plane-hopping full-time entertainer to desk-bound businessman is nearly complete. During the years of that transition I became surrounded by good people who have little or no idea about my previous life, and who certainly have never experienced the thrill of standing in front of an audience of spellbound strangers.

They cannot begin to comprehend the majesty of the moment I've just described.

But you can. Now I want you, if you haven't experienced it yet in your life, to get there as well, to the summit of that magnificent peak which can be reached by only one special kind of person—the entertainer.

You.

The Entertainer.

END